CREATIVE SCARECROWS
35 Fun Figures for Your Yard & Garden

CREATIVE SCARECROWS
35 Fun Figures for Your Yard & Garden

Marcianne Miller
with Merry Miller

LARK BOOKS
A Division of Sterling Publishing Co., Inc.
New York

THIS BOOK IS DEDICATED
TO THE MILLER TRIBE

Mary
Bobby & Pat
Murphy & Lynne
Michael & Cindy
Daniel, Jonathan,
& Mackenzie

ART DIRECTOR
Susan McBride

PHOTOGRAPHER
Keith Wright

COVER DESIGN
Barbara Zaretsky

ILLUSTRATOR
Merry Miller

ASSOCIATE ART DIRECTOR
Shannon Yokeley

ASSISTANT EDITORS
Rebecca Lim
Nathalie Mornu

EDITORIAL ASSISTANCE
Delores Gosnell
Anne Hollyfield
Rosemary Kast
Chris Winebrenner

EDITORIAL INTERNS
Robin Heimer
Kalin E. Siegwald
Ryan Sniatecki

LOCATION COORDINATOR
Jeff Hamilton

SPECIAL PHOTOGRAPHY
Evan Bracken, pp. 78, 123
John Dole, p. 92
Stephen J. Salmon, p. 32
Sandra Stambaugh, pp. 90,
97, 106
SANOMA SYNDICATION
Eric van Lokven, pp. 128–129
Jan Vermeer, p. 118
Hans Zeegers, p. 120

Library of Congress Cataloging-in-Publication Data

Miller, Marcianne.
   Creative scarecrows : 35 fun figures for your yard & garden /
Marcianne Miller with Merry Miller.-- 1st ed.
      p. cm.
   ISBN 1-57990-501-3
   1. Handicraft. 2. Scarecrows. 3. Garden ornaments and furniture. I.
Miller, Merry. II. Title.
TT157.M493 2004
745.5--dc22

                                                                    2003026267

10 9 8 7 6 5 4 3 2 1

First Edition

Published by Lark Books, A Division of
Sterling Publishing Co., Inc.
387 Park Avenue South, New York, N.Y. 10016

© 2004, Lark Books

Distributed in Canada by Sterling Publishing,
c/o Canadian Manda Group, One Atlantic Ave., Suite 105
Toronto, Ontario, Canada M6K 3E7

Distributed in the U.K. by Guild of Master Craftsman Publications Ltd.,
Castle Place, 166 High Street, Lewes, East Sussex, England
BN7 1XU
Tel: (+ 44) 1273 477374, Fax: (+ 44) 1273 478606, Email:
pubs@thegmcgroup.com, Web: www.gmcpublications.com

Distributed in Australia by Capricorn Link (Australia) Pty Ltd.,
P.O. Box 704, Windsor, NSW 2756 Australia

If you have questions or comments about this book,
please contact:
Lark Books
67 Broadway
Asheville, NC 28801
(828) 253-0467

Manufactured in China

ISBN 1-57990-501-3

Contents

Creative Scarecrows author
Marcianne Miller

Introduction

"I love your people!" the tiny trick-or-treating ballerina gushes as she holds up her basket for me to fill with Halloween treats. "She means the scarecrows," her mother says, indicating the dozen figures that dot my front yard.
"I love them, too!"

We laugh, and then, as naturally as the leaves fall around the pumpkins, the stories begin.
"Grandma always made scarecrows out of…"
"One summer, my father…"

Once again, a fondness for scarecrows makes friends out of strangers.

"Scarecrow" does seem an odd word for the life-size figures my family and I make every year. No matter how fierce I intend them to look, none of them ever really scares anybody, much less the bold and raucous crows. Truth is, my scarecrows attract birds!

They're like party guests—staying for a short while, amusing the adults and charming the children, demanding no long-term maintenance. More than any other kind of outdoor decoration, scarecrows bring vibrancy to a garden. Do you have an ordinary plot of land that you haven't landscaped yet? Put up a scarecrow and watch that space instantly become more colorful and inviting. New to the neighborhood? Display a few yard figures and soon you'll meet all the neighbors and their friends, too.

Throughout the pages of this book, you'll learn how to make all kinds of scarecrows and yard figures. Each one is different. One may appeal to your funny bone. Another could be your chance to show off your design skills. Others could be testaments to how well you can clean out your closets! No doubt you'll discover that making a scarecrow is more exciting than you ever imagined.

And the most important part of that discovery is the realization that when you make a scarecrow, you do indeed make something that seems to come to life. Your scarecrows may seem like real people to you. Shy, friendly, goofy, or in-your-face, your figures will acquire their own personalities, even give themselves names. This year alone, I welcomed the emergence of Babs Butterfly-Catcher, sexy Fredrico, Maid Marian, and Gonzo the Gargoyle. You'll meet them and more throughout this book—and I'm sure they'll acquire different personalities and names in your yard.

Like sand paintings and other ephemeral art, scarecrows by their very nature are short-lived. Usually set up in the summer or early autumn, rarely do they last until snowfall. What a good time, though, they pack into those few months—all those passers-by who do double takes and then drive back for another look, all the friendly over-the-back-fence conversations they instigate.

If you're a scarecrow maker, you were probably one of those kids who colored outside the lines. You like to work big, with broad strokes and bright colors that can be easily seen across long fields. You get a kick out of using what's unexpected, particularly things that other people have thrown away. Not having to worry about making a mistake that will last forever, you thrive on the chance to experiment to your heart's content.

Making scarecrows is a perfect craft for people who like to create without having to be perfect.

Creative Scarecrows illustrator and project designer Merry Miller

You don't need to be a good carpenter to make a scarecrow. In fact you don't even have to use a saw or hammer if you don't want to. You don't need expensive tools or materials—you can make perfectly wonderful scarecrows by crossing two broom handles and hanging shiny objects that twirl in the wind. You don't even have to have a garden—as you'll see, lots of scarecrows are perfectly at home on a porch or apartment balcony.

Seventeen wonderful designers made the projects for this book. They enhanced the traditional scarecrow-making process with experience from other creative fields: theater, painting, costume design, doll-making, gardening, welding—and watching lots of late-night movies! Some are full-time artists, others are creative newcomers whose work is making its first published appearance. In addition, you'll find examples of scarecrows from community festivals and art collections around the world.

My sister played a big role in *Creative Scarecrows*. I'm honored to share her inventiveness as well as the wealth of her hands-on advice. Her merry spirit permeates the book.

May you have as much fun making scarecrows as we did!

Crows, members of the *corvidae* family, are the most well known crop-eating birds.

Basics

Families, artists, gardeners, and neighbors in communities worldwide are exploring their creativity by making scarecrows and yard figures. This section covers the figures' fascinating roots and explains their basic construction principles so you, too, can join in the fun.

History of Scarecrows & Yard Figures

Ever since human beings started to grow food in an orderly fashion, birds have been trying to eat the plants first. In the beginning, early farmers scared the birds away by yelling and throwing stones. About 3,000 years ago in Egypt, farmers made a net device that caught the quail that were ruining their wheat crops. It was the first scarecrow.

Ancient Greek farmers built purple-hued statues of Priapus, a homely son of the god Dionysius, whose menacing glower in vineyards seemed effective against grape-stealing birds. The Romans, fond of imitating what was best about the Greeks, transported field statues to the lands they conquered, thus introducing the concept to the French, Germans, Swiss, and English, who in turn developed field figures in their own traditions.

On the other side of the planet, Japanese rice farmers were developing their own scarecrows.

Their first attempts were to string up dead fish on bamboo poles and burn the poles. The stench was so awful the birds stayed away in droves and the name *kakashi*, or stinky thing, came to be associated with any object that scared birds. More humanlike figures evolved, covered in reed raincoats with peaked hats.

Many centuries later, the English began creating figures stuffed with straw, topped by heads carved from turnips or gourds. Along with other European immigrants, the English brought their scarecrow customs to North America. Meeting them all across the continent were native bird-chasing traditions.

By the 1930s, the country cousin with painted face and patches on his overalls—what we now call the traditional scarecrow—was a common sight on American farms. In the 1939 *Wizard of Oz* movie, actor Ray Bolger sought a heart and made the straw-stuffed scarecrow an American icon.

Classic Japanese scarecrows aim arrows at offending birds. PHOTO COURTESY OF SATO SHINJI, JAPANESE SCARECROW SOCIETY

Modern garden dancers evoke ancient fertility figures.

Halloween, which occurs during harvest time, is often celebrated with scarecrows.

The traditional scarecrow is a favorite harvest symbol.
PHOTO COURTESY OF SCARECROW FESTIVAL, ST. CHARLES, ILLINOIS

9

Over time, scarecrows combined with statuary to create a hybrid form of popular outdoor art—yard figures—that are representations of humans, animals, and spirit beings. Developing rapidly from their early incarnations as kitschy garden gnomes and pink flamingos, yard figures are now fully respected, beautiful landscape sculptures. Unlike scarecrows, yard figures are meant to be long-lasting garden decorations, or made for special occasions any time of year.

Balloon figures are used for one splashy occasion.

Metal yard figures can last for many years.

Yard figures often resemble their statue predecessors.

Clay-pot animals are favorite small yard figures.

Like other forms of folk art that ordinary people have made and enjoyed without fanfare for decades, scarecrows and yard figures are now attracting the attention of serious art lovers. They are the subject of gallery and museum exhibits, and are sought after by folk art enthusiasts.

Yard art is a consuming passion for artist/collectors Jane Orleman and Dick Elliot of Ellensburg, Washington.
PHOTO COURTESY OF THE ARTISTS

For lovers of folk art, scarecrows are treasured sculptures.
COLLECTION OF CARL HAMMER GALLERY, CHICAGO, ILLINOIS, PHOTO BY JIM PRINZ

Though long removed from an agricultural economy, communities the world over have a deep-seated need to celebrate the harvest. Scarecrow festivals are beloved annual events, attracting tourists and fostering community pride and cooperation. In the process of creating scarecrows to share with others, families and neighbors come together for one last outdoor celebration before winter sets in.

Throughout *Creative Scarecrows*, you'll see snapshots of scarecrows and yard figures gathered from festivals in Japan, Switzerland, Canada, and the U.S., as well as from the work of individual scarecrow artists and collectors.

Community scarecrow festivals encourage local artists to show off their creativity.
PHOTO COURTESY OF MAHONE BAY SCARECROW FESTIVAL, NOVA SCOTIA, CANADA

Tools & Equipment

Most of the tools for making scarecrows you probably already have—a few power tools such as a drill and a jigsaw, and all the regular hand tools, such as pliers, wire cutters, hammer, and handsaw. For simple metal projects you'll need tin snips or an old pair of scissors. If you want to weld metal, you'll need access to welding equipment. For gourds you'll need a safety mask or respirator because gourd dust is toxic to some people.

Scarecrow-making hand tools are standard equipment in your home toolbox.

You'll need only a few power tools to make scarecrows.

SCARECROW-MAKING SAFETY

The usual commonsense safety rules apply when creating scarecrows and yard figures. Don't use a power tool unless you know how to. Wear protective glasses and gloves as necessary.

If you've got the scarecrow bug and it's pouring rain, can you build your scarecrow indoors? Sure, but keep in mind that the scarecrow might be larger than anticipated—look out for ceiling fans and low doorways. Also, these figures always seem to be heavier than you think. Get a buddy to help you haul and insert them into the ground. It's safer and more fun.

Materials

There is no limit to what kinds of materials you can use to make your scarecrows and yard figures. Our project designers used wood of all kinds, as well as salvaged auto parts, tin cans, umbrellas, copper pipes, balloons, pots of clay and plastic, and every imaginable type of fabric. Natural ingredients included bamboo, rattan, gourds, corncobs, lots of moss, and a whole feast of autumn nuts and fruits. The project instructions are full of many time-saving and weather-friendly products you can find in art and craft stores.

Gardeners love yard figures that use natural ingredients arrayed over metal frames.

This Pumpkin Shepherd is a combination of traditional figure-building materials and new products, such as durable synthetic pumpkins.

LUMBER: THE REAL DIMENSIONS

Lumber is cut at the mill in standard sizes, its *nominal* dimensions. A 1 x 2 is indeed 1 inch (2.5 cm) thick x 2 inches (5 cm) wide on its way to the mill. It leaves the mill, however, with an *actual* dimension of ³/4 inch (1.9 cm) by 1½ inches (3.8 cm), due to drying and milling procedures. (The milling process doesn't affect the length.) When precise lumber measurements are necessary, they are called for in the project instructions. Otherwise, the materials list will indicate the nominal lumber size, usually 1 x 2 or 2 x 2.

Making Scarecrows & Yard Figures

When planning to make your scarecrows and yard figures, there are four interconnected construction phases to consider. These are structure, stuffing, clothing and other coverings, and accessorizing. Each of these categories is discussed in the following sections.

Structure Basics

The basic scarecrow form is a simple T-cross, made from two pieces of lumber (or anything else), that are nailed, screwed, or tied together at the intersection. (See fig. 1 below.) Usually the spine is about 6 feet (1.8 m) high and the armboard about 4 feet (1.2 m) wide—of course, adjust either length as you wish.

All you do is cover the form with clothes (or something else), top it (or not) with a head, and hang things (or not) from the outstretched arms. In just a few hours, literally, you can create a yard full of scarecrows. The creative challenge with T-cross scarecrows is to work within the limits of the form while simultaneously expanding and enhancing it.

You'll see in projects throughout the book innumerable variations on the basic T-cross design—for example, armboards in hinged sections that allow more expressive gestures, hip bars that dramatize hanging fabric, double-spined forms for side-by-side couples, and X-crosses for cartwheeling figures.

The basic scarecrow form is a primitive human shape.

Figure 1: The T-cross frame is easy to build and decorate.

Cat Burglar and Kitty Thief demonstrate that you don't have to cover up the structure to make wonderful scarecrows.

Tea Party Lady shows why long dresses are favorite clothing for female scarecrows.

Butterfly Catcher's reach is gracefully extended with a pole and copper wire.

KID-SIZE SCARECROWS

Though most of the projects in the book are adult life-size or bigger, you can easily alter them to child-size by reducing the height and width. Cover the scarecrows in children's clothes, too. In fact, scarecrows make great use of last year's trendy clothes that no self-respecting kid would wear to school *this* year.

Lucy, the Opera Lover proves you *can* use those prom-night gloves and tiara again!

15

Yard figures have more complex forms than the scarecrow's simple T-cross. There are basically two classes of yard figures depicted in *Creative Scarecrows*: those built with simple geometric shapes, and those with free-flowing or natural lines, which are often made from thin metal, including poultry netting, such as in fig. 2 below.

Copper-Pipe Man & Poodle show off squares and rectangles.

Figure 2:
Yard figures with natural forms usually combine several techniques and a variety of materials. This rabbit head is shaped from a poultry netting frame over a simple wood armature. (See the Lucky White Rabbit on page 58.)

Umbrella Woman emphasizes triangles and circles.

Bamboo Wind Chime is a study in rectangles.

STRUCTURE SUPPORT

There's nothing sadder than seeing your beautiful scarecrow crashed face forward on wet leaves! That's why you always want to keep stability foremost in mind when making your figures. Avoid top-heavy designs. Use rebar to add support to spines—it's easily attached with wire, tape, or plastic ties. Weight figures as needed, such as with pebbles in shoes. Remember the destructive power of wind, and carefully secure attached parts, including hats and other items of clothing.

The standard rule for figures inserted into the ground is that there should be as much support below ground as one-third the aboveground height. For tall and/or heavy figures, dig postholes. See fig. 3 below for guidance.

Figure 3: Posthole
Add 4 inches (10.2 cm) of gravel, then backfill with dirt. The length of the post in the ground should be one-third the height of the post above ground. The width of the hole should be twice the width of the post.

Secure hanging figures with sturdy rope or wire. PHOTO COURTESY OF MARSHALL SCARECROW FESTIVAL, MARSHALL, MICHIGAN

Tall and/or heavy figures require postholes.

STRUCTURE ADDITIONS—
HEADS, HANDS, AND FEET

The most expressive parts of scarecrows and yard figures are the ones you alter or add on after you've made the basic structure. When designing projects for *Creative Scarecrows*, we attempted to present as wide a range of heads, hair, hands, and feet as possible. Here are just a few examples to prove that your choices are limitless.

Stuffing

For many people, especially in the U.S. and Canada, a scarecrow must be stuffed to be considered an authentic scarecrow. Stuffing a scarecrow is similar to making a big doll—you fill the figure's clothes with stuffing material, and close the openings in the clothes—usually hands and feet and shirt fronts—to keep the stuffing in. Usually you let a little stuffing stick out to show it off. Notice the difference between the unstuffed version of a scarecrow and the stuffed one in the photos at right.

Traditional stuffing is straw or leaves. Contemporary stuffing includes cotton batting, newspapers, and shredded paper—each wrapped in plastic trash or grocery bags or nylon stockings to keep them from deteriorating in the rain. No matter what you use, one rule seems to apply for all stuffing—you'll always need more than you think you do, so plan accordingly.

The unstuffed scarecrow has a spare, modern look.

The robust, old fashioned scarecrow proudly shows off his straw stuffing.

When planning your stuffing material—be creative—and think about things you can recycle.

Look-alike yard figures are built with a basic scarecrow form, then artfully stuffed with smooth materials to create a lifelike appearance. See the Junction City Jug Band on page 82 for tips on making custom-designed stuffing.

Plain nylon stocking faces can be shaped with simple stuffing and stitching techniques.

PHOTO COURTESY OF ST. CHARLES, ILLINOIS VISITORS BUREAU, BY KATHY SMITH

MAKING NYLON-STOCKING FACES

Stuffed nylon stockings make fascinating heads and faces. The traditional method is to manipulate the stuffing (usually soft cotton batting, which makes the smoothest stuffing) inside the stocking in the shape of facial features, and sew stitches as needed to make the shapes permanent.

You can also make three-dimensional features and sew them on. Fold over a little rectangle of nylon, stuff it with cotton and shape it into lips or eyes. Then color the features with permanent markers, and sew the pieces onto the face.

In either method, work in the thigh area of the stocking, keeping the ends of the stocking open so your hands can easily work from both ends. When the face is completed, knot the top of the head, and wrap the trailing piece around the spine. Knot the bottom and tie the tail onto the arm piece.

For distinctive faces, make separate stuffed and painted features, then sew them on.

Straw is the favorite material for scarecrow stuffing contests.

PHOTO COURTESY WISCONSIN DELLS AND CONVENTION VISITOR BUREAU

Another use of nylon stockings is to make bare arms and legs in sun-loving scarecrows.

PHOTO COURTESY OF MAHONE BAY SCARECROW FESTIVAL, NOVA SCOTIA, CANADA

POSES

No rule says scarecrows have to be inserted into the ground—you can attach them just about anywhere. Create figures, especially stuffed ones, to take any pose the human body can make—and more.

This stuffed scarecrow needs no internal support—he just hangs out on the boat.

PHOTO COURTESY OF MAHONE BAY SCARECROW FESTIVAL, NOVA SCOTIA, CANADA

Don't have much ground space? Let small stuffed figures climb up your porch railing.

PHOTO COURTESY OF MAHONE BAY SCARECROW FESTIVAL, NOVA SCOTIA, CANADA

Unexpected poses create dynamic scarecrows, as in this display at the Hershey Children's Garden, Cleveland, Ohio.

PHOTO COURTESY OF THE ARTIST, ALISON WILSON

Clothing & Other Coverings

Scarecrows happily wear any kind of clothing that you're not going to cry about getting soiled, sunburned, snagged, or snatched. Our project designers used every kind of material imaginable—flowered shorts worn 30 pounds ago, sparkly shower curtains, upholstery fabric, wool shirts the moths got to, burlap seed bags, kids' roller skates, Uncle Michael's suspenders, Aunt Edna's lace doily, cowboy boots worn one time on that ill-advised dude ranch vacation, a magenta taffeta dress somebody must have been loony to buy in the first place, loafers the puppy chewed...you get the idea.

The range of materials that you can use to cover yard figures is even wider. In addition to clothes and fabric, you can use natural ingredients of any kind, as well as just about anything man-made. Yard figures often bring out the environmentalist spirit, since many are made from or decorated with recycled and salvaged materials.

Accessorizing

I know for a fact that some scarecrow makers live for the opportunity every autumn to accessorize to their heart's content. It's those unique extra touches—the buttons, purses, hats, gloves, socks, sunglasses, jewelry—that take scarecrows from slapdash to fantastic.

Creating Characters & Scenes

By creatively combining all the elements of scarecrows—structure, stuffing, clothing and coverings, and accessories—you create figures that come alive. The secret to a good character figure is designing it with someone real in mind—a trick that automatically suggests expressive gestures, coloring, and the telling detail that captures the essence of the whole person.

The culmination of the scarecrow maker's craft is creating scenes, or vignettes, in which two or more characters capture a moment in time, like the freeze-frame in a movie.

It's easy to create humor when you have more than one figure in your design.

These musicians are portraits of the designer's family.

Tea party scenes encourage a charming variety of expression and fashion.

PHOTO COURTESY OF MAHONE BAY SCARECROW FESTIVAL, NOVA SCOTIA, CANADA

About the Projects

There are 35 projects in *Creative Scarecrows*, a lovely range of scarecrows and yard figures that you can make for your own garden. You'll see figures inspired by ancient Greek warriors and Native American legends, by French movies and Asian monsters, as well as typical American characters such as farmers, movie stars, and New Orleans jazz musicians. There's an amazing cast of characters—a pumpkin shepherd, a dapper gentleman, a wild woman, a welded warrior, two sisters on the neighborhood watch, four brothers in a jug band, and quite a few happy dancers. Yard figures aren't only human of course—there's a big bunny, a playful puppy, a glittery bug, two flashy flamingos, three gargoyles, a mermaid, an angel, a goddess, and a very eclectic fairy queen.

HAVE FUN!

Uncle Billy

Descended from a happy line of traditional scarecrows,
Uncle Billy is perfectly at home today in town or country.

Design by Merry Miller

INSTRUCTIONS

1 Sew the patches on the clothes.

2 Fold the burlap over horizontally. Cut about 14 inches (49.5 cm) from the left edge, and stitch up the two sides, making a rectangular pillow shape. Turn inside out so the stitches are hidden— and you've created a seam with the fold at the top of the head.

3 Cut eyes, nose, and mouth out of the felt. Sew on using big embroidery stitches.

4 Make the head's drawstring closure by threading the big weaving needle with a yard (.9 m) of twine. Don't knot it. About 5 inches (12.7 cm) from the bottom of the burlap bag, make big 1½-inch (3.8 cm) stitches around the bottom, leaving two long tails of twine on either side.

5 Completely stuff the head, press it down on the spine, and draw the twine closed to hold it in place.

6 Just as you did for the head, make big drawstring stitches on the bottom of the pant legs, leaving tails of twine. Stuff the pants and draw them closed.

7 Button or sew the shirtsleeves closed and stuff from the front until filled.

DESIGN TIP

The mouth of a scarecrow is the feature that creates the most expression in its face—and is usually the most difficult to design. You're always safe with a smile!

"I love scarecrows based on real people—this one was inspired by the stories my mother told of her beloved Uncle Billy in Junction City, Ohio."

—Merry Miller

MATERIALS

T-cross made out of 1 x 2 or 2 x 2 lumber
Old clothes
Assorted fabric squares for patches
1 yard (.9 m) of dyed burlap or traditional burlap
Felt for making features
Big buttons for eyes
Straw for stuffing
Embroidery thread
Twine

TOOLS

Big weaving needle
Sewing needle

Design by Merry Miller

MATERIALS

CLAY POTS
* 3 tapered bowls, 6 ½ inches (16.5 cm) high, for feet and neck (A)
* 2 "standard" pots, 8 ¼ inches (21 cm) high, for legs (B)
* 4 wide-lipped cylinder pots, 8 inches (20.3 cm) high, for legs

1 4-foot-long (1.2 m) sheet of ¾-inch (2 cm) plywood, for foot and torso bases and shoulders
Pencil
2 big white glazed foam pots for the torso (D)
3 wooden dowels, ¾-inch (2 cm) dia., 4 feet (1.2m) long
10 small synthetic pumpkins, for the arms
1 large synthetic pumpkin, for the head
Clear plumber's glue
Spray paint matching the clay and white pots
Wide black belt
10-lb (453 k) bag of pebbles or stones
25-foot (8 m) spool of 6 AWG (4 mm) copper wire
Garden gloves
Sheets of adhesive-backed felt in autumn colors and black
Straw hat
Fall leaf garlands (found in craft stores)
Shepherd's hook (found in garden supply stores)

TOOLS

Jigsaw
Drill with variety of bits, including a ¾-inch (2 cm) bit
Wire cutters
Round file
Sandpaper

Pumpkin Shepherd

Inspired by Basque shepherds, this raffish herdsman keeps a close watch on his pumpkin flock. Made with synthetic pumpkins, and designed in portable modules, he can be taken apart and reassembled year after year.

Before You Start

Often you'll be steadying the figure with one hand while you apply elements with the other, so set out all the materials within easy grasp.

INSTRUCTIONS

Cut Circles out of the Plywood

1 Trace the rim of the clay foot pot (A) onto the plywood, and use the jigsaw to cut out two circle bases for the feet.

2 Trace the rim of one of the white foam pots (D) on the plywood, add 2 inches (5 cm), and cut out two circles: one for the lower torso base, the other for the shoulder piece.

Cut the Dowels

3 You'll need two 3-foot (.9 m) lengths for leg supports.

4 You'll need one 25-inch (63.5 cm) length for torso support.

Drill Holes

5 Drill armholes, slightly larger than the diameter of the wire, on both sides of the upper torso pot (D), 3 inches (7.6 cm) below the rim.

6 Drill the same size holes into each of the 10 small pumpkins, through their stems to their bottoms.

DESIGN TIP

The synthetic pumpkins are carvable and keep their shape and color indefinitely.

29

Build the Legs with Four Clay Pots
(see fig. 1. on opposite page)

7 Glue the rims of the upside-down foot pots (A) to the wooden foot circles. Insert a 3-foot (.9 m) dowel into each foot pot, through the drainage hole. Really slather the glue on every time you glue, since you want to make a firm seal. You may have to widen the holes of the pots, as they are often irregularly produced. Use a simple round file or wrap coarse sandpaper around a pencil until it's thick enough to encourage larger holes.

8 Continue to glue the pots (as indicated, on their rims or bottoms), slide them down the dowel, and press them firmly on the pot below. Use fig. 1 to guide you in this sequence:
* Bottom of pot B
* Upside down rim of pot C
* Bottom of pot C

9 When all four pots are placed on the dowel and glued, the legs should measure about 25 inches (64 cm) tall, and the top of the dowels should stick out above them. Let every pot dry completely.

Build the Torso

10 Place the legs parallel to each other and about 2 inches (5 cm) apart at their widest section. Rest the wood torso circle on the dowels and from underneath, pencil mark where the dowels touch it. Drill two holes with the ¾-inch (2 cm) bit.

11 Prime the torso circle, then paint it to match the clay pots, which makes the legs appear longer. Let dry and slide it over the leg dowels.

12 Glue the rim of an upside-down white foam pot (D), and press it to the torso circle. Glue the bottom edge of the wide belt to the top of the upside down pot to hide the "seam" made when you position the next foam pot.

13 Set the second pot (D) on top of the first, bottom to bottom. Don't glue them together or they won't remain portable. To keep the torso steady as you work, weight the upper torso pot with the bag of stones.

14 Cut a hole in the center of the shoulder circle to accommodate the doweling. Prime and paint the circle white and set aside.

Make the Figure's Left Arm
(See fig. 1)

15 Cut a 12-foot (3.7m) length of wire, and bend one end of it into a hand shape, with a thumb on the inside of the hand.

16 Build the arm from wrist to shoulder, sliding the pumpkins down the wire, and changing their placement to make room for an elbow bend. Use fig. 1 to guide you in this sequence:
* Pumpkins #1 and 2 stem up
* Pumpkins #3, 4, and 5, stem down.

Make the Internal Arm-to-Arm Support (See fig. 1)

17 Temporarily set aside the bag of stones to give yourself room to work inside the pot.

18 Feed the loose wire end through the hole on the figure's left side, pulling the completed left arm tight against the torso.

19 Holding the arm in your right hand, with your left hand press and bend the malleable wire into the inside shape of the pot, making a U-shape down the left side, across the bottom and back up the right side and through the right side hole.

20 Put the bag of stones back in the pot, placing it firmly on the bottom to keep the U-shape of the wire.

Make the Right Arm Holding the Shepherd's Hook

21 Slide the pumpkins on the wire, this time going from shoulder to wrist, so it looks just like the opposite arm you built in step 16.

22 Make a right hand, remembering to keep the thumb on the inside.
Cut off any excess wire.

23 Cover both wire hands with work gloves.

Make the Neck & Head

24 Put the wooden shoulder circle on top of the upper torso pot (D). Push the 25-inch (63.5 cm) doweling through the circle and into the bottom of the pot. Glue the rim of the last tapered bowl (A), turn it upside down, and slide it over the dowel onto the shoulder circle; press and let dry.

25 Drill a hole into the bottom of the large synthetic pumpkin head, slather the bottom with glue, and fit it onto the dowel. Let dry.

26 Cut out and apply features, buttons, and finishing touches, from adhesive-backed felt, and press in place. Reinforce your shapes with additional glue if your figure will endure hard rains. Top with a quirky straw hat. Drape garlands around both circular bases.

27 Place the figure in the middle of a pumpkin patch. Insert the shepherd's hook into the ground next to the shepherd and wrap his hand around it.

"A man with a mustache—irresistible!"
—Merry Miller

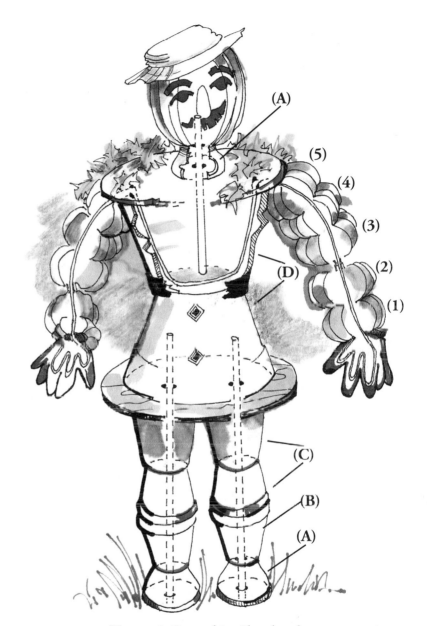

Figure 1: Pumpkin Shepherd

Wild Triangle Woman

From the state of Texas comes this flamboyant triangle woman. Make her shiny parts with holographic film backed with aluminum tooling—a unique combination that turns a simple design into a front yard conversation piece.

INSTRUCTIONS

Make the Body

1 Using the miter box and saw, cut the 2 x 2s into three pieces in three equal lengths of 18, 20, and 24 inches (45, 51, 61 cm) for a total of 9 pieces, each piece with a 60° right and left miter. Assemble the resulting triangles with small nails and wood glue. (See fig. 1 on page 35.) Sand, wipe clean, and prime with the white latex paint. Let dry and sand again, wiping clean.

2 Paint the spine 2 x 4 black, and set aside to dry. Paint the triangles, using the painter's tape to block edges if desired.

3 From the 1 x 2, cut a 24-inch (61cm) piece for the shoulders and four 12-inch (30 cm) pieces for the arms. Sand, prime, and paint.

Make the Hands

4 Using your hand as a template, add 1 inch (2.5 cm) all around, and draw two hands on the pine board. Prime, sand, and paint. Draw and cut out two hands on the tooling foil, and tack them to the wood hands at the edge of the wrists and ends of the fingers. (If you wish, emboss the foil, with a manicurist's orange stick, following the lines in your hands.) Drill a ¼-inch (6mm) hole about ¼ inch (6 mm) in from the center of the wrist edge, where you'll attach the hands to the arms later. Set hands aside.

Make the Eyes & Mouth

5 To make the eyes, cut a 7 x 9-inch (17.8 x 22.9 cm) piece of tooling foil, and roll it out flat. Remove the top edge of backing from a 6 x 8-inch (15.2 x 20.3cm) piece of silver holographic film, and place it on the tooling foil. Remove the rest of the backing, smoothing out the film as you apply it to the foil. Cut off excess foil. Draw two 2 x 2½-inch (5 x 6.4 cm) eyes. Cut out with craft scissors, and glue a jewel to the center of each eye.

6 Repeat the above process for the mouth, using the red film and the tooling foil. Draw an inside-mouth pattern on silver film. Peel off the paper backing, and place it on the red mouth, smoothing as you go.

Design by Sandy Whittley

MATERIALS

WOOD
* 2 2 x 2s, 8 feet (2.4 m) long, for 3 triangles
* 2 x 4, 8 feet (2.4 m) long, for spine
* 1 x 2, 8 feet (2.4 m) long, for shoulders and arms
* Scrap pine boards for hands

FASTENERS
* 6¼ x 2½-inch (6 mm x 6.4 cm) hexagonal all-thread bolts with nuts
* 12 lock washers to fit above bolts
* 12 2½-inch (6.4 cm) steel wood screws
* Box of ⁷⁄₁₆-inch (.11 mm) aluminum tacks

Wood glue
Sandpaper
¾-inch-wide (1.9 cm) blue painter's tape
White latex paint as primer and decorative paint
Acrylic craft paint, colors of your choice
Black latex paint for spine
1 roll of 36-gauge aluminum tooling foil (hobby shop)22 inches X 3 feet (55cm x .9m)
Adhesive-backed holographic film in a variety of colors (hobby shop)
Faux jewels
22-gauge brass wire, 75 feet (22.8 m) long
Blue twisted cord or ski rope
Small amount of clear silicone adhesive
2 CDs
1 package of large multicolored plastic beads (hobby shop)
Rebar

TOOLS

Radial arm saw, skill saw, or handsaw
Miter box set at 60°
Nail gun with small nails
Tack hammer
Screw gun
Electric drill with ⅛-inch (3mm) and ¼-inch (6mm) bits
Wrench to tighten nuts
Pliers
Measuring tape
1 or 1½-inch (2.5 or 3.8cm) paintbrush
Pair of old scissors
Small needle-nose jewelry pliers
Posthole digger

7 Using a small nail, tap two holes in the upper corners of each eye. Cut four pieces of brass wire 4 inches (10.2 cm) long. From the front, thread one wire through an eyehole, and use the needle-nose pliers to twist the wire around itself. Repeat for the other three wires and holes.

8 Tap tacks at 4 inches (10.2 cm) and 6 inches (15.2 cm) from both inside edges on the back side on top of the head triangle. Wrap each eye wire several times around a tack, making sure the eye hangs down with about 1½ inches (3.8 cm) of wire showing from the front. Hammer tacks in tightly. Cut off excess wire.

9 Using the above method, attach the mouth: tap holes in the sides and the bottom of the mouth; cut three 3-inch (7.6 cm) pieces of wire, tap two tacks on the back sides of the triangle 7 inches (17.8) up from the bottom point and one on the bottom point.

Make the Hair & Torso

10 Drill evenly spaced holes ½ inch (1.3 cm) deep across the top of the head triangle. Cut 23 pieces of blue cord, 6 inches (15.2 cm) long. Unravel each piece, leaving ½ to ¾ inch (1.3 to 1.9 cm) at the end. Put wood glue in each hole, stick in the unrolled end of cord, and continue across the head.

11 On each CD, carefully drill a ⅛-inch (3 mm) hole about ¼ inch (6 mm) in from the edge. Drill a pilot hole about 5½ inches (14 cm) from each top corner of the torso triangle, and tack each CD to the triangle at the holes. Set this triangle aside.

Decorate the Skirt

12 Make the tack sets to hang the decorations on the skirt triangle. On back bottom edge of the triangle, 2 inches (5 cm) from each side, lightly tap in a tack. Place other tacks, evenly spaced every 1½ inches (3.8 cm) across the bottom. Repeat on each of the backs of the two sides, lining up these tacks with corresponding tacks on the bottom to make 10 or 11 matching tack sets.

13 Using the same process as for the eyes and mouth, attach various colors of holographic film to tooling foil. Cut several lengths of 1inch (2.5 cm) wide strips of each color. Tap four evenly spaced holes in long strips, two in shorter strips.

14 Make as many decorative bead-and-foil sets, in various lengths, as tack sets. Use the diagram to guide you. Starting at bottom back outside edge, cut a piece of wire twice the length you think you'll need. Wrap the wire several times around the tack, and hammer in tightly. Working so you can see the front, thread beads and the foil on the wire. At the top tack, wrap the wire, and hammer down tightly. Repeat for all other wires, varying the number of beads, colors, and lengths as you like.

Assemble Pieces on the Spine

15 Center the bottom point of the head triangle 4 inches (10.2 cm) down on the spine, and attach with two wood screws. Note: it's much easier to screw from the front, but if you don't want to see the screws, attach them from the back.

16 Drill ¼-inch (6 mm) holes in each end of shoulder and arm pieces. With two wood screws, attach the shoulder piece to the spine about 2 inches (5 cm) down from the head piece.

17 About 2 inches (5 cm) down from the shoulder piece, carefully place the torso triangle. Wrap the CDs with protective rags or old toweling so you don't scratch them. Attach the torso triangle with two wood screws.

18 About 1½ inches (3.8 cm) from the point of the torso triangle, position the skirt triangle, and attach with wood screws.

19 Using hex-head bolts threaded with lock washers, put bolts through each end of the shoulder piece, then through the arms. Thread on other lock washers, and attach nuts on the back side. Repeat for the other side of shoulder, elbows, and wrists, working from front to the back. Position the arms the way you want and tighten in place.

20 If you wish, paint or decorate the black spine to indicate body lines and legs.

21 Dig a posthole. See instructions on page 17. Add rebar or a 3-foot (.9 m) wooden support post to the spine, and insert both. You can disassemble the post from the rebar and store the figure in the garage for the winter.

DESIGN TIP

Once you make this piece with its precise measurements, you'll have the techniques down pat so you can let loose with your next versions.

"You're going to put that thing in the front yard?" my husband said. We got so many compliments from our neighbors, now he loves it!"
— Sandy Whittley

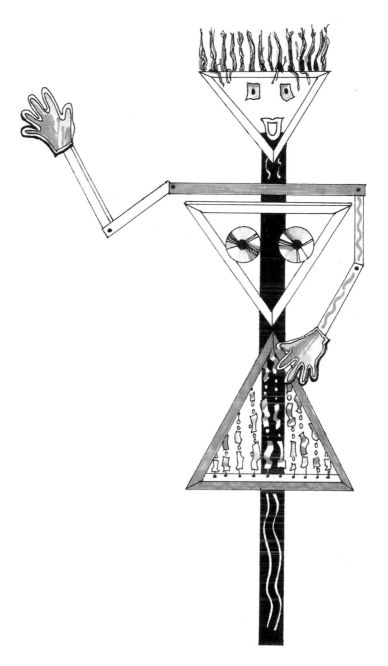

Figure 1: Wild Triangle Woman

Design by Joan K. Morris

MATERIALS

WOOD
* 1 section of 3-foot (.9 m) picket fencing with at least 6 pickets
* 5 feet (1.5 m) of rough wood slats, about 2 feet x ¼ inch (61 cm x 6 mm)
* Small piece of ½-inch (1.3 cm) plywood
* Small piece of ¼-inch (6 mm) plywood

FASTENERS
* 1½-inch-long (3.8 cm) wood screws
* Small nails
* 2½-inch-long (6.4 cm) corner braces
* 5-inch-long (12.7 cm) bolts, nuts, and washers
* 2-inch-long (5 cm) bolts, nuts, and washers
* Silver thumbtacks
* U-brackets to fit rebar

CLAY POTS ("TALL" SHAPE)
* 2 pots, 3 inches (7.6 cm) high, for woman's chest
* 3 pots, 4 inches (10.2 cm) high, for flower pots
* 3 pots, 6 or 7 inches (15.2 or 17.8 cm) high, for heads

Wood paint, your choice of color, plus cream, or yellow and white
Paint glaze
Oven-dry clay
Spray sealer
Industrial-strength glue
All-purpose craft glue
Jute
Eyeglasses
4-foot long (1.2 m) rebar for each clay-pot figure

TOOLS

Claw hammer
Jigsaw or handsaw
Drill with ⅛- and ¼-inch (3 mm and 6 mm) bits
Phillips-head screwdriver
Rolling pin
Garden shears
Staple gun
Tape measure
Pencil
Scissors
Wire cutters
Paintbrushes, 2 inch & 1 inch (5 cm & 2.5 cm)
Rags

Fence-Post Peekers

You'll always have neighborly neighbors with these convivial clay-pot people peeking over your fence.

INSTRUCTIONS

1 Use the claw hammer to remove every other slat from the fence section to make room to place the people. Save the removed pickets for the arms and the head ledges.

2 Turn the picket fence upside down so that the curved tops are on the bottom. Determine how tall above the back brace on the picket you want each clay-pot person to be, and saw each picket to that length.

3 Figure out how many slats you want for each person's torso. Then cut the slats so they're about 1 inch (2.5 cm) too long, and place them on the picket spine. Predrill two places on each slat, then drive in the wood screws. Continue this down the picket until you have the number of slats you want.

4 Pencil on the shapes of the torso sides, and cut them with the saw.

5 For arms, cut the removed pickets about 15 inches (38 cm) long, starting at the point of the picket.

6 For the head ledges, just behind the torsos, cut 5-inch (12.7 cm) sections from the remaining picket pieces. Attach the cut pieces with corner braces to the tops of the pickets.

7 To attach the arms, determine where you want them, then predrill and screw them in place from the front, using two screws.

8 To put the chest on the woman, predrill ¼-inch (6 mm) holes through the slats and a plywood backing. Run the 5-inch (12.7 cm) bolts through the center holes of the 3-inch (7.6 cm) pots and then through the drilled holes. Place washers and then nuts on the back and tighten.

9 Paint the torsos of the people with a base color and let dry. Give them a weathered look by making a mixture of 50:50 glaze and white paint, and using it as a wash over the painted figures. Paint it on, and then either rub off with a rag or use a graining tool to make the wood grain.

10 Mix a little cream or yellow paint into the mixture, and apply it to the remaining pickets.

11 Paint the head pots cream color.

12 Use the oven-dry clay to make the facial features and ears, following manufacturer's instructions. Roll out the clay with a rolling pin or by hand, and shape as you like. After they dry in the oven, paint the shapes, let dry, and spray with sealer. Glue to the pots with the industrial-strength glue.

13 Use the corner braces to attach the flower-pots to the hands. Screw the corner braces in place on the hands first, then place 2-inch (5 cm) bolts with washers and nuts through the holes in the bottoms of the pots and then through the corner braces. Tighten the nuts in place.

14 To attach the heads, mark through the holes in the bottoms of the pots onto the head ledge, and drill ¼-inch (6 mm) holes. Run 2-inch (5 cm) bolts with washers through the pot holes down through the ledge, and tighten the nuts.

15 To make ties, cut shapes out of ¼-inch (6 mm) plywood, and paint. Add silver thumbtacks to embellish. Nail in place with small nails.

16 Attach glasses by gluing them in place at the ears and the nose with craft glue.

17 Plant flowers or plants in the head pots.

18 Attach rebar to the fence posts with the U-brackets, and insert the bars into the ground, resting the fence posts on the ground surface.

DESIGN TIP

You can make cat and puppy figures, too, by modifying the facial features and ears and adding tails made from jute.

The more neighbors the merrier!
—Joan K. Morris

BAMBOO NEIGHBORS
Cut sections of
bamboo garden stakes
(or bamboo placemats)
with garden clippers
and shape the torso.
Adhere with industrial
strength glue or pre-
drill holes and drive in
small nails.

MOSS LADY
Cover a plywood torso
with grass cloth,
stapling in the back.
Wearing protective
gloves, use wire cutters
to cut out a section of
chicken wire to wrap
around the grass cloth,
also stapling it in back.

Stovepipe Hat Rocking Man

Back and forth the rocking man rocks, soothing everyone within his cheery gaze. Notice his jaunty old-fashioned stovepipe hat—made from the real thing.

Note About Welding

If you don't weld, you can still have wonderful metal figures in your garden. Gather all the metal parts, make detailed drawings of the figure you want, and take everything to a welder to fabricate for you—easy!

INSTRUCTIONS

1 Use the torch to cut off two leaf springs from the automobile springs. Ensure they both have the same curve radius so they will rock together.

2 Use the chop saw or torch to cut leg sections out of the rebar. Either weld two 3-foot (.9 m) pieces together or bend one 6-foot (1.8 m) piece in the middle.

3 Weld the rebar legs to the center of the leaf springs.

4 Cut three 16-inch (41 cm) sections of rebar. To the top of the legs, weld one piece for the body. Then weld the other two pieces to it, as arms, about 4 inches (10 cm) below the top.

5 Use the plasma cutter or the shears to cut the sheet metal into all the flat parts. Use whatever metal you have on hand, (The designer used 55-gallon [208 L] drum lids and an old clothes dryer.) Start with the pants and shirt. Cut and weld smaller pieces of metal on them to make patches or buttons, and then weld the clothes pieces onto the rebar body.

6 Cut out the hands and feet, and weld them to their limbs.

7 Cut out the head, and weld on other metal pieces for the features, such as a nose from bent sheet metal, eyes from railing end caps, and a mouth from half a horseshoe. Weld the head to the rebar body.

8 Weld the rain collar onto the stovepipe as a brim, and weld the hat onto the head.

9 Add colorful accessories, such as four metal cutout flowers welded to heavy wire and attached inside the hat. Attach metal fringe to the bottom of the pant legs with the hog rings.

10 Prime the sheet metal, and paint it. Add a raffia belt.

DESIGN TIP

For extra movement, weld store-bought coil springs to the rebar, and then weld the hands to the springs. Although worth the trouble, this isn't easy—springs can melt easily during welding.

Design by Bill Drake

MATERIALS

2 automobile leaf springs
Rebar, 1/2 inch (1.3 cm) dia., 10 feet (3 m) long
Sheet metal, enough to make all the parts of the figure
2 small springs approx. 6 inches (15 cm) long (optional)
2 metal tube railing end caps for eyes
Horseshoe or other metal for mouth
1 stovepipe elbow with rain collar for the hat
Heavy wire
10 hog nose rings
Cans of metal primer and paint
Raffia

TOOLS

Oxy/acetylene torch
Chop saw or hacksaw
Tape measure or ruler
Electric arc welder
Bench vise
Plasma cutter or metal shears
Pliers

SAFETY GEAR

Safety glasses
Welding gloves
Welding helmet
Leather apron
Protective boots

Vine Garden Sprites

Small rattan-wrapped sprites dance with abandon under your favorite tree.
They begin life with the most simple frames—made of clothes hangers.

MATERIALS
for One Sprite

6 clothes hangers

15 pieces of 18-gauge copper wire, each about 6 inches (15.2 cm) long

1 hank of vine rattan, with the bark on or off (found in basketry supply shops)

1 steel rod, 36 inches (91.4 m) in length

TOOLS

Strong pliers

Wire cutters

Scissors

Water for soaking the vine

INSTRUCTIONS
for One Sprite

1 Make the arms and legs by elongating four of the hangers, using figs. 1 and 2 on page 44 as your guides. Smooth out any lumps, shaping the hangers into long ovals with the hooks at one end.

2 Make the body out of the fifth hanger, making a more rounded shape, as in fig. 3 on page 44.

3 Make the head from the last hanger. As in fig. 4 on page 44, pull, then twist it about 4 inches (10.2 cm) around to make a head at the top end, and the hook at the bottom.

4 Connect the hangers by wiring them together with the copper wire pieces. Take the body, hook up, and place the arms over the chest area, hooks at the end for hands. Cross each arm hanger over the other one across the width of the chest area, then wire them down to the body, as in fig. 5 on page 44.

5 Wire the leg hangers to the bottom of the body, with their hooks down, as if they were feet. Straighten all five hooks.

6 Put the round head up in between the arms with the hook down between the legs (as in fig. 5). Anchor it with copper wire. Then bend the hook up between the legs into the body area, and secure with wire. Finish the frame by using the 18-gauge wire to secure any loose areas. The frame should be rigid.

7 Soak the hank of vine rattan in water, about 10 or 15 minutes until pliable. Keep the bark on or peel it off, depending on what color you want (see design tip below). Starting with the body frame, anchor the beginning of the vine to it, then randomly wrap the vine, in and out, until you get a secure first layer of vine over the entire frame.

8 Continue to wrap, being sure to weave in and out of the existing vines to tighten the wrap. Since the frame is basically flat, it's your wrapping that gives the dancer dimension. Just wrap more vines in the areas you want to accentuate.

9 Thread one end of the metal rod up through a leg and into the body, then stick the other end into the ground. The figures will be self-standing.

DESIGN TIP

If you leave the bark on the rattan vines, they stay their earthy color. If you take off the bark, the dancers are so pale they glow in the moonlight.

Because these figures are so easy to make they become inspiring introductions to the art of basketweaving. —Mary Hettmansperger

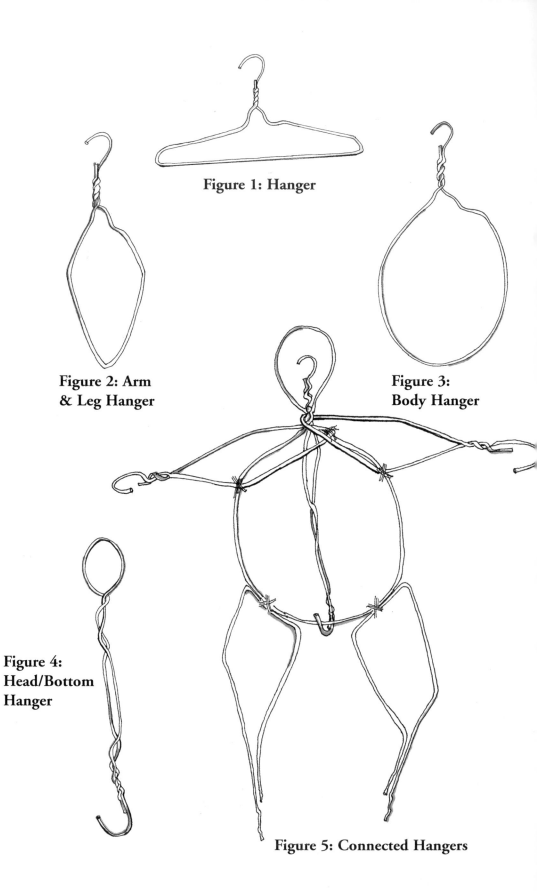

Figure 1: Hanger

Figure 2: Arm & Leg Hanger

Figure 3: Body Hanger

Figure 4: Head/Bottom Hanger

Figure 5: Connected Hangers

Scarecrows love showing happy faces, no matter what their bodies seem to be doing!

PHOTOS COURTESY OF MAHONE BAY SCARECROW FESTIVAL, NOVA SCOTIA, CANADA

Clay-Pot Puppy

This puppy tickles your funny bone every time you see him.
Clay pots of different sizes make his expressive body; rope holds him
together and makes his fuzzy tail.

Before You Start

Work on a tabletop, covered with soft cushioning, such as old towels, in case you
drop the pots. It takes some practice to hold the pots at the same time you're feeding rope through their holes.

INSTRUCTIONS

1 The figure of the puppy, with its parts labeled, is on the next page.
Use it to guide you through all the steps.

2 Place the two body pots (A) on the table, top rim to top rim. Temporarily tape
them together, which will help you line up the holes you'll drill next. Using the
ceramic bit, drill about eight holes in each pot, evenly spaced about ¾-inch (1.9
cm) below their rims. The holes should be as wide as the rope you'll use to lace the
two body pots together later. Drill two more holes into each pot, about 3 inches
(7.6 cm) from the pots' bottoms, where you'll later connect the legs. (See fig. 1 for
this step and throughout.)

3 The crouching hind legs are composed of two sections: the upright part, which
is two pots (B) and (C) rim to rim, and the foot, pot (D), attached at a right
angle. Drill a hole in the side of the bottom pot, pot (B), about 1-inch (2.5 cm)
from its bottom. Feed an 18-inch (45 cm) length of rope through the hole. Make a
huge knot (two or three ties at least) on the outside of the hole. (Later this knot will
support the dog's foot, pot (D).

4 Weight the hind leg pots, but leave the rope sticking up out of the pots while
you do. Cut a plastic bag to fit inside pot (B), leaving enough to fold over and
seal later. Fill it with pebbles and pack it in the pot, around the rope, until the pebbles are flush with the rim. Staple the bag closed.

5 Thread the other end of the rope loosely through the hole of pot (C). Repeat
the weighting process ion step 3. Glue the rims of the pots and press them
together, keeping the rope taut inside the pots and a long tail coming out pot (C).
Let them dry.

6 Tie a final sturdy knot on top of pot (C).

Design by Merry Miller

MATERIALS

ASSORTMENT OF CLAY POTS IN
"STANDARD" & "TALL" SIZES

* 2 "tall" pots, 7½ inches (19 cm)
high, for body (A)
* 4 "standard" pots, 3 inches (7.6 cm)
high, for tops of legs (B)
* 4 "tall" pots, 4½ inches (11.4 cm)
high, for bottoms of legs (C)
* 4 "standard" pots, 1½ inches
(3.8 cm) high, for feet (D)
* 1 "standard" pot, 2¼ inches
(5.7 cm) high, for snout (E)
* 1 "standard" pot, 4½ inches
(11.4 cm) high, for head (F)

Tape
4 yards (3.6 m) of sisal or hemp
rope, with diameters appropriate to
the drain openings of the pots
Small plastic bags for holding pebbles
Pebbles for weight
Clear plumber's exterior glue
20 gauge wire
1 piece of scrap 2x2, 2½ inches
(6.3 cm) in length, cut to 45°
angle on one end
1 black stone for the nose
2 pieces of black leather or vinyl
for the eyes
Leather scraps for ears

TOOLS

Drill with ceramic or concrete bit
Wire cutters
Stapler
Scissors

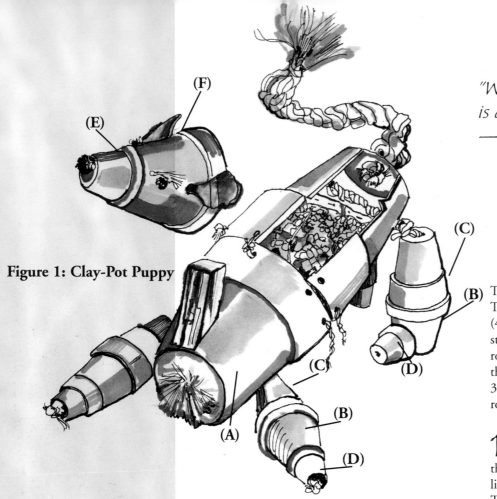

(F)

(E)

Figure 1: Clay-Pot Puppy

(C)

(B)

(C)

(D)

(A)

(B)

(D)

"What every clay-pot puppy needs is another puppy to play with!
— Merry Miller

(B) Tie a big knot on the inside of the pot and glue. To shape the tail, put a crimp on an 18-inch (45.7 cm) piece of 20-gauge wire and push the straight end through the hole. Braid or wrap the rope strands around the wire and shape it. To fluff the tail, wrap wire around the rope strands about 3 inches (7.6 cm) from their ends and unravel the rope up to the wire.

7 Thread the remainder of the rope through the hole in the side of the back body pot (A). Knot it on the inside of the pot, pulling the leg section firmly against it.

8 Thread the rope through the other side of the body pot (A) and make another secure knot on the outside.

9 With the remaining rope, reverse the leg-building process in steps 4 and 5 and make the opposite hind leg.

10 Glue the foot pots (D) at a right angle onto each leg and let dry.

11 Make the tail. Cut three strands of rope about 18 inches (45.7 cm) long. Push them through the drainage hole of the puppy's back body pot.

12 In similar fashion as you made and attached the hind legs, make the front legs, except that you don't have to weight them because they lie flat. (Don't stuff the front legs with pebbles. To insure that the puppy will always stay in a play position. He can't stand up without weighted front legs).

13 Stuff the body with pebbles. The front body pot will require more weight but it will shift naturally when the body is laced together. Fill two bags with pebbles and place one in each of the body pots. With rope (or any other strong lacing material) lace the pots together, starting at the belly.

14 Make the internal head support. Glue the angled edge of the 2 x 2 onto the front body pot (A). (See fig. 1 above left.) Let dry.

15 Make the puppy's head. Glue the rim of pot (E) to the bottom of pot (F) Let dry. Glue on the nose and eyes as well as the ears. (cut scrap leather pieces to make ears, and add "furry" rope eyebrows.)

This life-size pot-man is a combination of clay and plastic pots, strung together with sturdy knotted rope. Flowers and moss give him extra "living" touches. PHOTO COURTESY MAHONE BAY SCARECROW FESTIVAL, NOVA SCOTIA, CANADA

Gordalia Gourdie is the height of gourd fashion at the Cleveland Botanical Garden Festival in Ohio.

PHOTO COURTESY EVA PAWLAK, HIGHLAND HEIGHTS GARDEN CLUB

Gourd Triplets—Bud, Blossom, and Tendril—took first place at the Cleveland Botanical Garden Scarecrow Festival. PHOTO COURTESY EVA PAWLAK, HIGHLAND HEIGHTS GARDEN CLUB

*Design by
Joan K. Morris*

MATERIALS

MIRRORS

20 1-inch (2.5 cm) dia., for the sunburst

26 2-inch (5 cm) dia., for the sunburst

2 2½-inch (6.3 cm) dia., for the palms

1 mirror tile, 12 inches (31 cm) square

1 hubcap or wheel cover about 8 inches (20 cm) in diameter

Wooden trellis, 6 feet (1.8 m) high

1 piece of ½-inch (1.3 cm) plywood, the diameter of the hubcap

4 pieces of ¾-inch (2 cm) plywood, cut to 15 inches (38 cm) each, for arm sections

1 x 2, 8 feet (2.4 m) long, cut to length as needed, for the spine

4 flat aluminum rods, ½-inch (1.3 cm) wide, 8 feet (2.4 m) long

Silver spray paint

48 thumbtacks

5 2-inch-long (5 cm) bolts, with nuts and washers

1 5-inch-long (13 cm) bolt, with nut and washer

2 3-inch-long (8 cm) repair braces

Industrial strength craft glue

1-inch-long (2.5 cm) wood screws

TOOLS

Jigsaw

Hacksaw

Drill

Drill bits: ¼-inch (6 mm) wood, ⁵⁄₃₂-inch (4 mm) metal

Screwdriver

Tack hammer or small hammer

Pencil

Measuring tape

Hubcap-Retro Trellis Man

Mirrors and a salvaged hubcap transform a store-bought trellis into a retro-style sculpture.

INSTRUCTIONS

1 Trace the perimeter of the hubcap onto the ½-inch (1.3 cm) plywood, and cut it out with the jigsaw.

2 Measure the trellis from the bottom to the top, add 6 inches (16 cm), and cut the 1 x 2 spine at this length.

3 Spray the fronts and backs of the trellis, the spine, and the plywood circle with the silver paint. Let them dry.

4 Use the hacksaw to cut the aluminum rods into six pieces each in the following four measurements (a total of 24 pieces):
 * 15 inches (38 cm)
 * 12 inches (30 cm)
 * 9 inches (23 cm)
 * 6 inches (15 cm)

5 Use the metal bit to drill two holes into the end of each piece.

6 Using the photo to guide you, arrange the aluminum pieces on the wood circle in a sunray design. Start with the 15-inch (38 cm) pieces spaced evenly, then fill in with the remainder. Attach each piece with a thumbtack in each of its two holes.

7 On the wood circle, measure and mark two holes: one in the center and another 1 inch (2.5 cm) below it. Drill the two holes with the ¼-inch (6 mm) wood bit.

8 Line the 1 x 2 spine up with the bottom of the trellis running up the center back, leaving 6 inches (15.2 cm) above its top on which to attach the hubcap head. From the front of the trellis mark, drill four ¼-inch (6 mm) holes about every 2 feet (.61 m) through the trellis and the spine. Place 2-inch (5 cm) bolts into the holes from the front of the trellis through the spine, and secure with washers and nuts.

9 Position the drilled wood circle as the head on the top of the spine. Mark and drill the spine where the two holes line up from the circle of wood. Run a 2-inch (5 cm) bolt through the bottom hole of the wood circle into the spine and secure with a washer and nut

10 Place the hubcap over the wood circle, and run the 5-inch (13 cm) bolt from the front of the hubcap through the center hole of the wood circle and into the spine. Secure with a washer and nut.

11 Lay the trellis on the ground, and using the photo on page 51 to guide you, arrange the two sizes of round mirrors on the aluminum rods. Glue them and let dry.

12 Place the mirror square in the center of the trellis, mark its location with pencil lines and glue it. Let dry.

13 Make the arms. Using the wood bit, drill holes through the ends of the arm pieces, and connect them with wood screws into a bent-elbow shape. Place the arms onto the trellis, using the two repair braces; drill and screw them in place. At the end of each arm, glue one of the big round mirrors to look like the palm of a hand.

DESIGN TIP

Use flat aluminum rods, not round aluminum poles, because they are much easier to cut, drill, and glue.

"An auto junkyard turned out to be a gold mine of salvaged metal treasures."
— Joan K. Morris

Gruesome Gourd Gargoyles

The gruesome gourds clack and rattle like dried bone skeletons—the neighborhood trick-or-treaters giggle in terrified glee.

Design by Joan K. Morris

MATERIALS
for Three Gargoyles

Assortment of 3 gourds, for the heads
3 1 x 2s, 4 feet (1.2 m) long, for the spines
Wood slats, 2 inches (5 cm) wide, about
20 feet (6 m) in total length, to cut for
shoulders and arms (see Cutting List below)
1 package bamboo garden stakes
3 pairs of large google eyes on springs
(found on novelty eyeglasses in party
stores)
Black and white spray paint
Clear polyurethane spray
3 corner braces, 2 inches (5 cm) long
6 bolts, 1 inch (2.5 cm) long, with nuts
and washers
12 wood screws, 1-inch (2.5 cm) long
12 binder rings, 2-inch (5 cm) dia., for the
hands and elbows
18 binder rings, 1-inch (2.5 cm) dia., for
shoulders.
1 package 1-inch (2.5 cm) brad nails
Spool of 5-ply jute
Hot-glue gun and glue
Raffia
Spanish moss
Sandpaper

CUTTING LIST: Wood Slats

3 pieces 20 inches (50.8 cm) long, for
shoulders for all 3 figures
12 pieces 8 inches (20 cm) long, for 4 arm
sections for each figure

TOOLS

Pencil
Protective glasses
Rotary tool with bit or keyhole saw
Long spoon
Drill
Pliers
Screwdriver
Handsaw
Hammer
Scissors

SAFETY GEAR

Dust mask or respirator

Before You Start

1 Wear a protective mask or respirator when working with gourds.

2 Clean the gourds outdoors. Use warm water and a stiff brush to remove some of the dirt and mold, but leave enough imperfections to keep them scary. Allow to dry.

INSTRUCTIONS
for Three Gargoyles

1 Make the heads, putting stems on top or facing forward as the noses. Pencil on the faces, making the mouths big enough to allow you to clean out the insides. Carefully use the rotary tool or keyhole saw to cut out the face, making the eye hole the size of the spring of the google eyes.

2 Use the long spoon to scrape out the loose material and seeds.

3 Spray the insides with black spray paint, a little at a time until covered.

4 Spray the outside of the gourd with the clear polyurethane and let dry.

5 Make the neck brace. Mark on the gourd where the two holes of the corner brace will be and drill holes. Attach the corner brace with the bolt from the bottom of the gourd through to the inside of the gourd head, place a washer and nut on it and screw tight with the pliers.

6 Spray the 1 x 2 spines with black spray paint. Let dry. Attach each to the corner brace on the bottom of each gourd, and brace them with the wood screws.

7 Make the shoulders. Use the wood screws to attach the 20-inch (50.8 cm) slats horizontally 4 inches (10.2 cm) down from the tops of the spines. Drill holes 1 inch (2.5 cm) from the end of each shoulder and placed low enough on the slats so the ring binders can go through them. Drill two more holes at each end—2 inches (5 cm) apart—from which to hang the torso bones.

8 With the handsaw, cut the bamboo in appropriate lengths to create the rib cage and hanging bones. (Use the photo on page 53 to guide you.) Predrill holes in the center of the bones, and hold in place with the small brad nails.

9 Drill holes in each end of the arm slats, and attach them to the shoulders and elbows with the 2-inch (5 cm) ring binders.

10 Spray all the bamboo pieces with white paint to look like bones. It won't hurt to over spray onto the rest of the figure; in fact, it makes them look creepier.

11 Starting at the base of the neck, hot-glue one end of the jute, and wrap it around the spine and torso, hot-gluing every couple of inches. When you get to the ribs, crisscross with the jute, and keep wrapping it down a couple of feet, and hot-glue the end.

12 Hot-glue the ends of the google eyes to the eye sockets.

13 Add hair by drilling a hole in the top of the gourd large enough to run the raffia through, and glue in place.

14 Hot-glue the moss from the shoulders and bones.

DESIGN TIP

Make the gargoyles even scarier by placing luminaries underneath them to cast flickering shadows.

"Boo!"
— Joan K. Morris

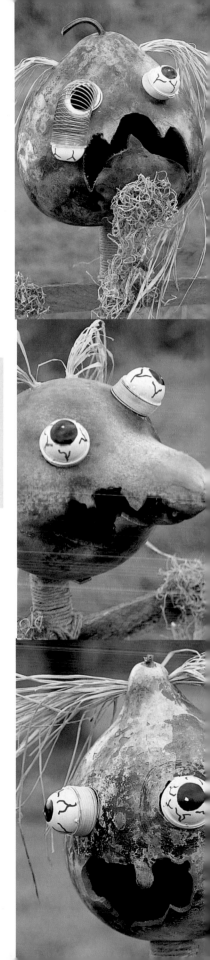

The first scarecrow festival in Denens, Switzerland was a small local affair. It became so popular that now it's an annual event, attracting tourists from all over. The scarecrows and yard figures are large and wildly creative, with a frequent use of recycled materials.

ALL PHOTOS ARE COURTESY OF SOCIETÉ DE L'EPOUVANTAIL, DENENS, SWITZERLAND

Design by Merry Miller

MATERIALS

20 white kitchen trash bags, size "tall"

Pine shelving board, 8 inches (20.3 cm) wide, at least 26 inches (66 cm) long

Scrap 2 x 2, 8 inches (20.3 cm) long

Scrap 1 x 2, 6 inches (15.2 cm) long

Wood screws or nails

4 sturdy plant supports, each 5 feet (1.5 m) high

2 sections of rebar 4 feet (1.2 m) long, painted white

Protective gloves

Roll of poultry netting (chicken wire), hole diameter of 1 inch (2.5 cm)

Small spool 20-gauge galvanized wire

Can of spray adhesive

Bow tie, your choice of color

Sheet of adhesive-backed black felt

TOOLS

Scissors

Drill and bit to match plant support diameter

Handsaw

Hammer

Screwdriver

Rubber mallet

Sledgehammer

Tin snips or wire cutters

Staple gun

Pencil with eraser tip

Lucky White Rabbit

Affirm your good fortune for all to see with this snowy rabbit and his shamrock-green bow tie. His statuesque shape is a poultry netting frame over the simplest wooden armature; squares of white plastic make his rain-friendly fur.

INSTRUCTIONS

1 Prepare a small flat area in your garden to assemble the rabbit in place.

2 Use the scissors to cut the kitchen trash bags into about 400 5 x 5-inch (13 x 13 cm) squares. Cut on the fold so the pieces are doubly thick.

3 Cut the shelving into two pieces: 15 inches (39 cm) long for the shoulder piece; 11 inches (28 cm) long for the statue base. Drill one hole in each corner of the two pieces. (See fig. 1 on page 61.)

4 Make an armature for the rabbit's head in the shape of a backward sloping numeral 7. (See fig. 2 on page 61.) Cut a 45° angle at the top edge of the 2 x 2 scrap. Nail or screw its flat end to the center of the shoulder shelving piece. Nail the scrap 1 x 2 on the angled 2 x 2 piece, making the nose support.

5 Make the frame of the statue (see fig. 1), a long narrow rectangle, wider at the top. With the rubber mallet push the four plant supports through the holes in the shoulder board, flush with its top. Pound the other end of the supports flush with the bottom of the base board.

6 Sledgehammer the two white rebars 12 inches (30 cm) into the ground, leaving at least 3 feet (.91m) above ground. Line the bars up with the holes in the wooden base. You'll wire the completed rabbit frame to the rebars later.

7 Shape the rabbit's head. Using the tin snips, cut a strip of poultry netting, about 20 x 8 inches (51 x 20 cm). Drape the wire over the armature from front to back, and staple it to the top of the nose piece. Shape the rest of the head one section at a time, cutting pieces to fit as you go. Use the figures to guide you.

"Use the same construction principles to design a garden lion or elephant—or a statue-worthy friend."
—Merry Miller

8 Make the ears one at a time, starting with the straight ear. Roll a piece of netting about 13 x 9 inches (33 x 23 cm) into a tube, using the loose wires to make a closed seam. Twist the loose wires at the bottom into the wires on the head, and secure them. Use additional wire if needed. Shape the top of the ear by pinching in the sides. To make the bent ear, cut a longer piece of poultry netting, about 20 x 9 inches (51 x 23 cm). Roll it, secure it, and shape it into a roguish tilt.

9 Cover the top of the shoulder piece with sections of poultry netting, cutting the wire to fit. Staple the wire to the wood. Curve the sections slightly so there's enough room to fill the holes later with the plastic squares.

10 Cut 5-foot (1.5 m) sections of netting from the roll, and starting at the left side of the rabbit, staple the top of the netting to the shoulder and the bottom to the base. Using the loose wires down the sides of each section, twist the wires to attach them to one another. If needed, use the 20-gauge wire to secure the pieces. (If you want to wire on the bow tie, leave a section of the back uncovered, so you can reach inside.) Cut, wrap, and staple all four sides.

11 Gently move the frame into position. Use the 20-gauge wire to secure the two back plant supports to the two rebars that you positioned in step 5.

12 Starting at the head, insert the plastic squares over the entire rabbit. Spray the adhesive both on the netting and on the backside of each square. Turn the square over so the unglued side is facing you, then use the eraser end of the pencil to push the center of the square through a netting hole. Work one small section at a time, being careful not to over-spray the adhesive. You'll quickly find out not all holes have to be stuffed as each plastic square spreads over a few holes. It takes time to spray each plastic square, but doing so will ensure that they will stay in place no matter what the weather.

13 Attach the bow tie by looping a piece of wire on the back of the tie's knot and threading the wire through the front of the rabbit. Reach from behind and twist the wire to secure it.

14 Add poultry netting to the open area in the back, then fill it in with the plastic squares.

15 Cut out two eye shapes from the black felt, and glue them.

16 When all the holes have been filled, stand back and take a good look. Trim uneven sections with scissors. Rake up any errant pieces of plastic because they're harmful to birds.

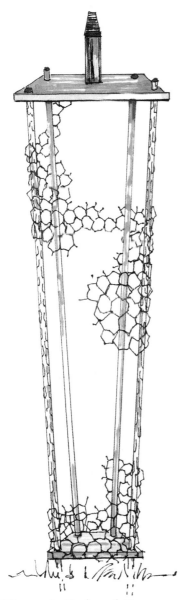

Figure 1: Pedestal Frame

Figure 2: Head Armature & Frame

One-Man Band

With his tomato cage conga drum and wind-blown music, this one-man band will jazz up any spot in your garden. Make him from a cast-off chair, a few cat food cans, old spoons, and fabric from last year's Halloween costume.

Design by Merry Miller

INSTRUCTIONS

1 The type of chair you choose determines your design possibilities. The designer's chair back was high, so she made her figure tall and lean. A shorter chair would make a plump figure or one that is child-size. If you're lucky enough to have a complete chair, then use it, modifying it as desired. If your chair, like this one, has a seat but no legs, make legs from other salvaged wood.

2 To make the arms, use pieces from other furniture, or cut and attach 2 x 2s. Screw in corner braces to make sturdy right angle arm bends.

3 For the legs, use any salvaged furniture pieces, or make new ones. The conga drum supports the figure, so you don't have to make a back leg, especially since it's hidden from view by the drum. But do add a pole or wood support to balance the chair. Cut a piece that is the length of the musician's lower leg; nail or screw it at an appropriate spot on the figure. Paint flat black so it seems to disappear.

4 The front right leg in this design is prominent and needs a solid structure. Make the thigh from metal corner molding (that already has handy holes for hanging noisemakers) and attach a cut 1 x 3 as the lower leg.

5 Cut a 2 x 2 to length for the neck. Screw it to the chair and tilt it as you like. Create the illusion of a face structure by simply intersecting scrap 1 x 2s and screwing them on the back of the neck. Add painted stones as eyes.

6 Decorate and paint your musician.

7 Make a hat out of the reed wastebasket, cover it with fabric, and hang bells.

8 Use whatever noisemakers you have on hand, such as bells left over from holiday decorations. Or make your own. Punch holes in the tops of tin cans with an awl or nail and hammer. Thread wire, nylon line, or twine through the holes, attach them to the leg on one end and knot them inside the noisemakers on the other.

9 Make the conga drum from the tomato cage. Wire or sew bits of fabric or leather onto the cage. Keep the look airy, especially if you want real plants to grow up the cage and add even more color. Insert the bottom prongs of the cage (at the narrow end) firmly into the ground all the way to the first horizontal section, then place the figure in such a way that his arm is on top of the cage, drumming it.

DESIGN TIP

Gluing brightly colored cloth is a simple way to add decoration. Spray adhesive to attach the cloth pieces to the wood as you work out your design, then use all-weather glue to attach them permanently.

MATERIALS

Salvaged wooden chair

Pine boards, 2 x 2s or 1 x 2s to cut for arms, neck and leg supports, as needed, at least 8 feet (2.4 m) total

1 x 3, approx. 3 to 4 feet (.9 to 1.4 m) long, if needed, for musician's lower leg

Metal corner molding, 3 to 4 feet (.9 to 1.4 m) long, if needed, for musician's thigh

Corner braces of appropriate size

Cans of spray primer and flat black

Cans of enamel spray paint, your choice of colors

Masking tape

Tomato cage for conga drum

Brightly colored fabric remnants

Screw eyes

Wood screws of appropriate length

Twine, string, ribbon, as needed

Assorted metal cans, clean with labels remove

Reed waste basket

Adhesive spray, hot glue, or all-weather glue

Noisemakers, such as old spoons, bolts and washers, chimes and bells

TOOLS

Saw

Drill

Screwdriver to fit screw heads

Tin snips

Awl

"This character represents what jazz means to me—bright colors and spontaneous movement on a solid geometric structure."
— Merry Miller

Flutter Bug

Design by Stacey Budge

A jewel bedecked bug sparkles in the sun as his fluttery wings shoo away other critters.

MATERIALS

1 decorative banister post, at least 5 feet (1.5 m) high

2 PVC pipes, ½-inch (1.3 cm) dia., 8 feet (2.4 m) long

4 yards (3.7 m) light-weight colorful fabric

Matching thread

Copper wire

All-weather glue

Paint and decorations for the body

4 cup hooks, 1½ inches (3.8 cm) long

Wood preservative (optional)

TOOLS

Scissors

Needle and thread or sewing machine

Drill

Posthole digger

INSTRUCTIONS

1 Cut the fabric into two lengths of 2 yards (1.8 m) each. With right sides facing, cut big scallop shapes on the edges so the wings will drape nicely.

2 Sew a 1½-inch-wide (3.8 cm) seam, leaving an opening at the bottom edge of the wings in which you'll insert the PVC poles later. Hem all the raw edges.

3 Paint and decorate the butterfly body as you like—go nuts! Leave the bottom 12 inches (30 cm) unpainted or treat the area with wood preservative.

4 Drill a hole in the top of the butterfly post. Shape copper wire into antennae and glue them into the hole.

5 To support the wings next to the body, attach the cup hooks at the top and mid-point on the back of the post.

6 Run the PVC pipes through the wing seams. Press the poles, now covered by the fabric, into the cup hooks—which will tear a hole in the fabric, like a buttonhole. Once the wings are in place, glue the perimeter of this hole so it won't get bigger.

7 See posthole digging instructions on page 17, then dig a hole and insert the butterfly.

DESIGN TIP

The wings are terrific canvases for fabric art techniques such as batik and tie-dye.

"Colorful Tibetan prayer flags inspired this project. They always looked like wings to me."
—Stacey Budge

Polka Dot Dancers

Polka dots! Is there anything more summery? Add dots galore to simple stick figures who sway like salsa dancers in the sunset breeze.

Design by Merry Miller

INSTRUCTIONS for Both Figures

1 To design the figures, measure yourself to get fairly accurate arm and leg measurements, then add a few inches to achieve an exaggerated dancer look. Use wider boards for some sections of the male dancer to give him an attractive masculine contrast to the slim lady dancer. (See the photo.)

2 Working on the ground, position one piece of wood over another until the arrangement strikes your fancy. Make a pencil line at the overlapping angles. Use the miter box saw to cut each piece. The irregular pieces contribute to the designs' illusion of movement.

3 Decide which parts of the dancers you want to be movable so you can adjust them to create gestures. For example, the lady's head can tilt, and her arms swing left or right. The man's arms, legs, and head can also be repositioned. Using the photo as a guide, predrill and countersink all the holes.

4 Paint everything with white primer and let dry. Then paint all the solid colored parts, and set them aside to dry.

Make the Lady Dancer

5 Press the circular coding labels on the dress sections, spray the wood fluorescent pink paint, and let dry. Peel off the dots, revealing the circles of white paint underneath.

6 Use wood joiners and wood glue to assemble the odd-angled sections of the dress, which will remain rigid and give the figure stability.

7 Screw each elbow to its upper arm; the neck and head to the shoulder. Glue and screw each assembled arm to its shoulder and each leg to the dress hem.

8 Staple the pinwheel hair decoration. Add screw eyes underneath the shoulder, and use fishing line to attach the metal circles.

Make the Male Dancer

9 His shirt has two kinds of dots-white donuts and solid blue. Press the white adhesive hole reinforcements securely on the shirt sections (which have been primed white). Then spray dark blue and let dry. Without removing the hole reinforcements, press circular coding labels in between them. Spray over fluorescent green and let it dry. Peel off all the adhesive circles. Voila! You have perfect circles in two colors!

10 Screw and glue the shoulder and hip sections to the torso. Place the shoulder piece behind the torso and the hip in front of it-creating another illusion of movement. Screw and glue the upper arm sections to the shoulder: the inside arm in front of the shoulder, and the outside arm behind the shoulder. Screw the elbows on each arm. Screw on the leg assembly in the same manner as the arms, inside leg on the front of the hip, and outside leg behind it.

11 Thread the wire through the necktie to make it look as if it's flapping in the wind. Prime the tie with the white spray, and let it dry. Use the fabric or floral paint to give it the final color. Let it dry, then tie it around his neck.

12 Screw the head into the torso, above the tie, and angle it jauntily.

13 Place two screw eyes in the shoulders of each figure, close to the ends. Hang the figures where they can catch the passing breezes.

"You don't need a tree to have garden dancers—I attached several dancers on a stretched clothesline—they looked spectacular."—Merry Miller

MATERIALS

3 1 x 2 pine furring strips, 8 feet (2.4 m) long

1 x 3 pine board, cut to length, for man's shoulders

2 x 2 pine board, cut to length, for man's torso

Pencil

Wood screws

Wood joiners, as needed for tough angles

Wood glue

Screw eyes

1 can white primer spray

3 cans fluorescent spray paint: pink, yellow, and green

2 cans enamel spray paint: dark red and royal blue

Adhesive reinforcements for punch-hole paper (found in office supply stores)

Adhesive circular labels (found in office supply stores)

Pinwheel or other hair decoration for lady

Metal can lids for lady's torso

Fishing line

20-gauge wire, to stiffen the necktie

Necktie

Fabric or floral paint

Small corkboard or wooden frame for man's head

TOOLS

Miter box

Miterbox saw

Drill

Countersink drill bit

Screwdriver

Flamingo Balloons

*Design by
Pamela Owens*

Who says you can't be totally outrageous? Flashy pink flamingos warn everyone what a wild party this is going to be!

MATERIALS
for One Flamingo

5-inch (12.7 cm)
BALLOONS
* Pink, approx. 150
* Yellow, approx. 100
* Black, 4
* White, 4

2 10-foot (3 m) sections of ¼-inch (6mm) dia. aluminum rods
1 section of ½-inch (1.3 cm) metal conduit, 3 feet (.9 m) long (found in home supply stores)
Conduit cap to fit conduit
Duct tape
Cardboard
Foam core about 10 inches (25.4 cm) long (found in craft stores)
Can of black spray paint
Cool-glue gun and glue sticks
Yellow adhesive circular labels (found in office supply stores)
Accessories such as bow tie or boa

TOOLS

Hacksaw
Electric balloon inflator or air compressor, or hand pump (found in party supply stores)
Craft knife

BEFORE YOU START

Work in a large flat area to build the frames and attach the balloons. If you don't have a van or truck to transport the finished figures, you'll need to assemble the figures in place.

INSTRUCTIONS

1. Using the figure on page 70 to guide you, cut the aluminum rod sections with the hacksaw. Use the strength of your bent knee, if needed, to mold the shapes. Duct tape the sections together to form one continuous frame, overlapping the tape about 3 inches (7.6 cm) per section. The tape can easily hold the lightweight rods.

2. Cap the conduit to keep out dirt and pound it into the ground. Insert the frame into the conduit.

3. Cut a 3-inch-wide (7.6 cm) hole in a piece of cardboard to use as a sizing template. Inflate the balloons two at a time, starting with the yellow ones, size them to 3 inches (7.6 cm), and tie their ends together. (See photo 1 on page 70.)

4. Twist two pairs together to form a cluster of four balloons. (See photo 2 on page 70.)

5. Starting at the bottom of the frame, slide the balloon cluster down, positioning it so that the two bottom balloons are on either side of the frame. Twist the two bottom balloons around each other once to hold the cluster in place. After you've done this a few times, it will be as easy as tying your shoe. Continue until you've covered the frame.

ABOUT BALLOON YARD FIGURES

You can make your balloon figures up to two days ahead of time, storing them in a cool place. Balloons start to oxidize in sunshine after a few hours; they'll remain fully inflated for two to three days, depending on the weather.

Balloons are made of latex, a rubber by-product. Thus if some fly away, you don't have to worry—they're biodegradable.

"We're never too grown up to love balloons!"
— Pamela Owens

6 With the craft knife, cut the beak from the foam core. Spray it black, and press into place among the balloons. Use cool glue (not hot!) to adhere it in place. Add the yellow adhesive circle on the eyes.

7 Add accessories as you wish, making sure they rest lightly against the balloons or blow in the breeze.

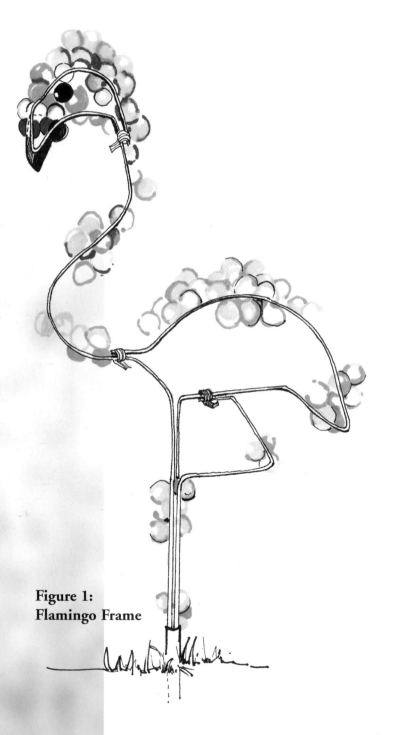

**Figure 1:
Flamingo Frame**

Photo 1: Tie ends together.

Photo 2: Twist two pairs into a cluster.

70

Women scarecrows love dressing to the nines and showing off all over town. PHOTOS COURTESY OF MAHONE BAY SCARECROW FESTIVAL, NOVA SCOTIA, CANADA

Design by Merry Miller

Waterfall Woman

On sunny days, her shower curtain gown shimmers like falling water. When it rains, her pitcher funnels water into the waiting birdbath.

MATERIALS

2 2 x 2s, 8 feet (2.4 m) in length

2 plastic pitchers, for the head, and for pouring

Shower curtains, your choice of watery colors

Wood screws or nails

2 right-angle corner braces

Small scrap of ³/₄-inch (1.9 cm) plywood for bird perch (optional)

Cans of white primer spray and watery colors of lavender, aqua, silver, and dark blue

Aluminum pie tin to make facial features

Clear exterior plumber's glue

¹/₂ inch (1.3 cm) diameter rebar, 4 feet (1.2 m) long

Wire or plastic ties

Birdbath

TOOLS

Drill

Screwdriver

Hammer

Saw

Staple gun

Scissors

INSTRUCTIONS

1 The figure in the photo is 5 feet (1.5 m) tall, in proportion to the small, low birdbath. Adjust the instruction measurements to the height of your birdbath.

2 Cut one 2 x 2 to 6½ feet (1.9 m) for the spine.

3 Cut the other 2 x 2 into two 16-inch-long (40.6 cm) sections to make the shoulder bars. Attach them horizontally and parallel, about 11 inches (28 cm) from the top of spine, in front and in back. (See fig. 1 at right.)

4 Cut a 14-inch-long (35.6 cm) section to make the pouring arm and position it between the shoulder bars (see fig. 1). Nail or screw the arm so it stays permanently angled. Make a pitcher holder by screwing the two right angle corner braces side by side, 1 inch (2.5 cm) from the arm's bottom. (This placement will vary according to your pitcher shape and handle.)

5 Cut a 16-inch (40.6 cm) section to make the upraised arm and attach it between the shoulder bars. Cut a round bird perch from scrap plywood, and nail it to the arm.

6 Prime, paint and let dry.

7 Make the dress with wavy strips of shower curtain fabric. Drape them full length—from hem to ring hole—on the shoulder bars, then cut to length. The more irregular the strips, the more they'll look like falling water. Glue or staple the strips in place.

8 Cut features from the pie tin and adhere them to the face pitcher with the plumber's adhesive. Glue narrow strips of shower curtain to the top for hair. Screw or nail the head to the spine.

9 Insert the rebar into the ground, and attach it to the figure's spine with wire or sturdy plastic ties. Move the birdbath into place underneath the pouring arm.

10 Cut a hole in the top side of the pitcher. Rain will fall into the hole and flow through the spout into the birdbath. On sunny days, create the illusion of flowing water by gluing narrow strips of silvery fabric to the inside middle of the pitcher so they cascade out of the mouth.

DESIGN TIP

Hang darker strips on the back shoulder bar to create the illusion of depth. Congregate the lightest strips in the front and center.

Figure 1: Waterfall Woman

Design by Harry Abel

MATERIALS

BAMBOO

* 1 broom made of bamboo twigs (or see broom instructions at right)
* 1 section of bamboo wider than the broom handle, 24 inches (61 cm) long, as sheath
* 2 bamboo branches, for arms and fingers
* 4 poles, 4-inch (10 cm) dia., 30 inches (76 cm) long, for shoulder and hip pieces, and 2 legs
* 2 poles, 1½-inch (3.8 cm) dia., 8 feet (2.4 m) long, for wind chimes

Rebar, ½-inch (3.8 cm) dia., 3 feet (.9 m) long
4 chopsticks
Black poly twine
Construction glue or equivalent

TOOLS

Miter saw
Cutting tools such as hand pruner, handsaw, hand sickle
Drill
Drill bit set
Calipers (to measure diameters)

Bamboo Wind Chime

Every piece of this giant wind chime is bamboo. The designer promises its clack and rattle will "scare the black out of a crow!" If you're not a crow, however, you'll love the exotic music and imagery it calls to mind.

HOW TO MAKE A BAMBOO BROOM

MATERIALS

Branches and twigs of about 5 growing canes of golden bamboo (phyllostachys aurea)
1 bamboo pole, 1-inch (2.5 cm) dia., 5 feet (1.5 m) long
Copper or steel wire

INSTRUCTIONS

1 Cut the canes off the culms (or stems) with a sharp pruner or hand sickle, and make a 3-inch (7.6 cm) diameter bundle of the twigs.

2 With the wire, tie the twigs together at their base around the top end of the pole, allowing the branches and twigs to go every which way.

GENERAL INSTRUCTIONS

1 Insert the rebar halfway into the ground. Slip the bamboo sheath over the top of the rebar. Slide the broom handle down into the sheath above the rebar, so the sheath tightly holds them both. Test the fit, then set the broom aside.

2 Make the shoulder out of one the wider poles, determining where it should sit on the broom handle (approximately 6 inches [15 cm] below the end of the twig bundle). Drill a hole through the shoulder to match the diameter of the broom handle where it meets the shoulder (approximately 1¼ inches [3.1 cm]). In both sides of the shoulder piece, every 3 inches (7.6 cm), starting at the ends, drill ¼-inch (6 mm) holes, from which you'll hang the ribs later.

3 Slide the handle of the broom through the center hole of the shoulder piece, adjusting it as you make space on the handle for the neck. Just under the shoulder, drill a ¼-inch (6 mm) hole through the handle and insert a chopstick as a pin to hold the shoulders onto the broom handle. Put the handle back into the sheath.

4 Make the hip piece from another section of the 4-inch (10 cm) diameter bamboo. Follow the same procedure as steps 2 and 3.

5 Make 16 wind chime sections, 10 to hang from the shoulder, six to hang from the hip. Try to cut about 1½ inches (3.8 cm) above a node, which is the little swelling on the culm, or stem. You will need:

* 2 lengths at 18 inches (45.7 cm)
* 2 lengths at 15 inches (38 cm)
* 4 lengths at 12 inches (30 cm)
* 4 lengths at 9 inches (23 cm)
* 4 lengths at 6 inches (15 cm)

6 Drill a ¼-inch (6 mm) hole through both sides of each wind chime, about ¾ inch (1.9 cm) from the top end.

7 Hang ten chimes from the shoulder piece with knotted black twine, using the photo as a guide for placement. Let each chime hang freely about 3 inches (7.6 cm) down from the shoulder.

8 To the outer edge of the hip piece, hang the two remaining 4-inch diameter (10 cm) poles to look like stubby legs. Repeat the process in step 7 to hang the remaining six hip chimes.

9 Glue two scrap pieces of the 4-inch diameter (10 cm) poles together side by side, as eyes. Then glue two pieces of smaller diameter bamboo inside them as eyeballs. Let dry. Insert two chopsticks horizontally through the base of the broom handle to serve as pins, then slide the eyes over them and glue. You can make ears in the same way.

"Working with bamboo, I feel connected to ancient craftsmen."
— Harry Abel

10 Naturally growing *phyllostachys* bamboo has two "branches" coming off each node. (Actually, this is how to identify *phyllostachys* from the other bamboos.) Select two sections for arms with the branches intact. Prune the branches to about 6 inches (15 cm) each for the fingers. Caliper the first two culms, and drill holes of this diameter in the top of the shoulders, near the opposite ends. Insert the ends of the culms into these holes, making two upright arms with horrifying hands.

DESIGN TIP

There's no waste when working with bamboo. Every piece ends up serving an artistic purpose.

Autumn Garden Fairy

The fairy queen gleams, a perfect match for the glorious autumn leaves around her.

INSTRUCTIONS

Decorate Both Skirt Pots

1 Spray the ochre and the yellow paint over the lace onto the pots. With the rag, rub bronze and gold paint over them, creating a lovely autumn glow. Let them dry.

2 Create a beaded wire hoop to fit around the rim of the upside down bottom pot, twisting the ends of the wire in the back to secure it.

3 Create the decorative girdle that hangs from the upside down top skirt pot. Pound the forks and spoons flat, then use the pliers to curl the fork prongs. Drill holes in their handles. Out of thick wire make the hoop, then use the thin wire to thread the utensils onto it.

Make the Torso

4 Paint the shoulder block and all the surfaces of the crate, inside and outside, as you did the pots in step 1, and let dry.

5 Place the open crate on its side, lengthwise. Using the ⅞-inch (2.2 cm) bit, drill holes through the centers of what are now the top and bottom of the crate, as well as the center of the shoulder block. The dowel will slip through these holes later to hold the entire figure together.

6 Create decorations inside the crate so they'll be peeking through the slats of the crate when it's closed. Add fence hooks inside the crate to hang the decorations.

7 Close the crate lid. Weave vines and wire in and out of the slats, avoiding the center where the dowel will pass.

Design by Emma Pearson

MATERIALS

CLAY POTS
1 big pot, 14 inches (35.6) high, for lower skirt
1 basin pot, 12 inches (30 cm) wide, for top skirt
1 "standard" pot, 17 inches (17.7 cm) high, for head

COPPER AND TIN
* 2 spools of thin copper wire
* 2 spools of thicker copper wire
* 2 copper piping attachments for elbows
* 1 pack of small piping attachments for crown
* 1-foot-long (30.5 cm) piece of copper piping, wide enough to slide over the dowel
* 2 large tin cans

WOOD
* Block of wood, approx. 14 x 4 inches (35.6 x 10.2 cm) for shoulders
* Wood crate or slatted box, approx. 10 x 6 inches (25.4 cm x 15.2 cm) for body
* Wooden dowel, ⅞-inch (22 mm) dia., 4 feet (1.2 m) long

PAINTS AND DECORATION
* Piece of old lace
* Cans of yellow and ochre spray paint
* Blue acrylic paint for face, red for lips
* 1 bottle of bronze acrylic enamel paint
* 1 bottle of gold acrylic enamel paint
* Fence tacks
* 20 to 30 forks and spoons
* 1 pack of large glass beads.

Bricks to serve as a base, approx. 12 inches (30.5 cm) square
Vines with berries
4 branches, approx. 1½ inches (3.8 cm) in dia., 5 inches (12.7 cm) long, for arms

TOOLS
Rags
Wire cutters
Hammer
Pliers
Drill with ⅞-inch (22 mm) drill bit, and small bits for wood and metal
Paintbrushes
Pruner to cut branches
Tin snips
Rasp, file, or coarse sandpaper for shaving the dowel

Make the Arms

8 Drill holes in the top and bottom of each branch. Thread wire through the holes into the copper fittings to make elbows, connecting the two arm pieces on each side.

9 Drill holes through the shoulders, and attach the arms with copper wire. Link all the pieces together with wire.

10 With tin snips, cut out two hand shapes from tin cans, and drill holes in the wrist. Thread wire through the holes in the hands and the lower arm branches to attach them. Paint fingertips with copper paint.

Assemble the Figure

11 Prefit the dowel from the head, through the shoulder and crate and skirt pots, into the ground, shaving as needed.

12 Stack up all the pieces on the bricks, from bottom up, sliding them down the dowel. Push the dowel firmly into the ground, leaving enough on top on which to place the head.

13 Slip the 5-inch-long (12.7 cm) piece of copper pipe over the dowel to make the neck between the shoulders and the head pot. With the fine brush, paint the face in blue acrylic on the head pot.

Make the Wings

14 Shape a wing-size figure eight with the thick copper wire, making two wings that join in the middle. Bind and wrap with the thinner wire, then randomly weave in wire and beads across the edges of the wings. With a fence hook, hammer the wing unit onto back of shoulder piece, making sure the wings are secure.

Add the Royal Touches

15 Make the wand, wrapping thick copper wire with thin wire and beads, as you like. Weave wire on the hand and wrist to attach the wand, adding beads if you want to make it a bracelet. Shape her fingers around the wand handle. Glue small pipe connectors around the edge of the head pot to make a shiny crown. Add vines and berries to the hole in the top of her head, giving her a high, dramatic headpiece.

DESIGN TIP

Keep the fairy adorned with wreaths of native berries so she'll reign through winter, feeding the hungry birds.

"Because I come from Wales, I love fairies...
I want them everywhere in the garden, don't you?"
—Emma Pearson

Scarecrow festivals in Japan are popular community events. In addition to being big and vibrant, many scarecrows are subtle satires on political issues. The Kaminoyama Hot Springs National Scarecrow Festival has been celebrated for more than 30 years.

Junction City Jug Band

Design by Merry Miller

How perfect for players in a jug band to have heads made of jugs! Attention to detail and smooth stuffing make the figures lifelike; straw bales provide a unifying visual theme as well as needed support.

MATERIALS

4 empty gallon milk jugs
Adhesive-backed felt (found in craft stores)
Clear exterior plumber's glue
Small pieces of burlap
Cans of spray paint for hair colors
2 6-foot-long (1.8 m) 1 x 2s
2 6-foot-long (1.8 m) 2 x 2s
Wood screws
4 bales of straw
Clothing for the four characters
Small pieces of hook-and-loop tape
Needles and assorted thread colors
Thimble
Newspapers for stuffing
1 roll of plastic tall kitchen bags
Plastic grocery bags, as needed
4 pairs of work gloves
4 Rebars
Pebbles for weight

TOOLS

Handsaw
Jigsaw (optional)
Drill
Rasp/file
Screwdriver
Hammer
Coarse sandpaper

BEFORE YOU START

1 The easiest way to make realistic faces is to use photographs of people you know. (The designer used her three brothers and brother-in-law as models—and now she has to make figures for everyone else in the family!)

2 Use old musical instruments if you have them. If not, cut them out of plywood, like the fiddle the designer made.

INSTRUCTIONS

1 Make the eyes, eyebrows, and mustaches by cutting adhesive-backed felt, reinforced with plumber's glue. For the hair and beards, combine burlap pieces sprayed with paint.

2 Make the armatures of the seated and partially seated figures, as in fig. 1 on page 85, out of 1 x 2 spines, cut to 40 inches (1 m) long.

3 For standing figures that use the straw bales only for partial support, such as the fiddle player, use full-length 2 x 2s cut to 5 feet (1.5 m) in length. You'll need to add a rebar support later.

4 Shave the ends of the spines with a rasp, file, or coarse sandpaper to fit them into the narrow mouths of the jugs and slip the jugs on the spines.

5 Make the horizontal shoulder supports out of 1 x 2s, 14 to 16 inches (35.6 to 40.6 cm) long. Screw them behind the spines, directly underneath the head as in fig. 1 on page 85.

6 Stick the spines for seated figures firmly into the straw bales, as in fig. 1. Create visual interest by placing the bales in different positions.

7 Hang the shirts on the shoulder pieces, then place the pants and overalls (overalls help hold stuffing in place). Attach the pieces of clothing with pins or needle and thread.

8 If your characters have as much body language as these do, use this method to create smooth stuffing. Fold up newspapers, like the wrapping of a deli sandwich, in lengths that approximate real limbs, as in the sequence in fig. 2 on the opposite page. Wrap the folded newspapers in white plastic trash bags, and stuff up the shirtsleeves and pant legs until you achieve the fullness you want, as in fig. 1. For the torsos, make big rounded pillow-shapes of newspaper, wrap in plastic trash bags, and push them inside the shirts. Use wads of newspaper, as in fig. 3, wrapped in plastic grocery bags, to fill in as needed.

9 Add additional clothing pieces, such as suspenders, belts, vests, and or jackets. The more layered the clothing, the more realistic the figures become.

10 In look-alike vignettes, hands become as important expressive elements as the faces. Plan the placement of each finger, depending on what instrument is being played. Making one hand at a time, stuff each finger of the glove with tiny rolls of newspaper, as in fig. 1. For fingers that need to be permanently bent in shape, such as on the flute player's hands, sew the fingers in position. Stuff the palms of the gloves, then sew the gloves onto the shirtsleeves.

11 Add shoes and boots underneath the pant legs, adding more stuffing to the legs if necessary, and weighting the footwear with pebbles.

12 Add hats, matching kerchiefs, sunglasses, or any other accessories that real musicians favor. Add pumpkins and old-fashioned cider jugs to the display.

Figure 1: Seated Player

Figure 2: Fold newspaper to make smooth stuffing.

Figure 3: Wrap wads of newspaper in plastic to fill in stuffing.

85

Silverware Woman

Rescued silverware and an old wooden window become an expression of
vintage elegance. Add shiny dryer-hose pantaloons for a touch of hardware chic.

*Design by
Nathalie Mornu*

INSTRUCTIONS

1 Adjust the instruction measurements to fit the
window and other parts you have. The six-paned
window in the photo is about 28 x 20 inches (71 x
51 cm), which is a nice size for a long, slim torso.

2 Determine the length of the neck board, being
sure to make it long enough to show off what
you choose to use as a head. Cut the board, and
screw it to the top center back of the window.

3 Determine the length of the leg boards. Add at
least one-third the aboveground height of the figure to have enough to insert into the ground. Saw a
point at the bottom end to help drive the legs into
the ground later.

4 Screw the flat ends of the legs to the bottom
center back of the window, about 6 inches (15.2
cm) apart.

5 With the craft knife, cut the dryer hose in half.
Pull one half of the hose over each board leg.
Secure it by stapling it to the window or the board
leg, whatever looks best.

6 Drill holes for the connector hose arms, sized
to hold the hose tightly, then secure them with
the epoxy.

*"I look at this figure in my
yard...so old yet so lovely... and
everything seems all right..."*
—Nathalie Mornu

7 Use epoxy to attach the handles of the ladles
together to make the halter strap, and attach
them to the window with the wire.

8 Into the front of the window, drive nails
from which you'll hang all the implements.

9 Drive the scarecrow into the ground so it's
secure. (If you're using rebar on the two legs,
see the tips on page 17.)

10 Using the photo as a guide, hang two
rows of knives from looped wire to create the fringe at the bottom of the window.

11 Attach wire to the spoons and four forks,
then hang them.

12 Use wire to attach the remaining forks to
the strainer head, leaving an empty area in
the front for the face. Screw the head to the top
of the neck.

DESIGN TIP

Lots of metal objects—bells, cooking
utensils, nuts and bolts, railroad spikes,
and other salvaged metal—look
wonderful hanging in yard figures.

MATERIALS

Old wooden
window frame

3 boards, cut to length
as needed for neck and
two legs

8 feet (2.4 m) of dryer
hose (found in home
improvement stores)

2 flexible metal connec-
tion hoses (found in
the plumbing section)

Nails and screws, as needed

Epoxy

2 old ladles

20 or so old knives

4 old spoons

32 old forks (4 hanging
from the window,
28 on the head)

100 feet (30.5 m)
of 28-gauge wire

Deep-fry strainer or similar
metal object for head

2 sections of rebar, as
needed (optional)

TOOLS

Saw

Drill and bits, as needed

Craft knife

Stapler

Hammer

Wrench

Wire cutters

Aluminum Mermaid

Design by Diana Light

She glows at poolside, waiting for the right light to reflect her wonderful self... ah, mermaids...shouldn't you have one at least once in your life?

MATERIALS

Template, enlarged to 20 inches (51 cm) across (Fig. 1 at right)

Aluminum flashing, 20 x 45 inches (51 x 114 cm)

Masking tape

Permanent marker

A few sheets of self-adhesive vinyl (clear)

Pencil

Outdoor spray paints in copper and blue

Copper mesh

Weather resistant glue for metal

Copper foil, ¼-inch (6 mm) thick

Shiny baubles for eyes, mouth, and bellybutton

Faux pearls

TOOLS

Scissors

Cutting mat

Craft knife

"My mermaid reminds me of what I'd rather be doing." —Diana Light

INSTRUCTIONS

1 Enlarge the mermaid template to fit the width of the flashing. Tape it to the flashing, and trace around it with the permanent marker. Use scissors to cut it out, just inside the marker line.

2 Cover one side of the mermaid with the self-adhesive vinyl. Pencil in the interior lines: arm, hair, face, and fish scales. Go over the lines with the permanent marker.

3 Place the mermaid on the cutting mat and use the craft knife to cut away the areas to be painted, then cut through the aluminum for interior areas in the neck and arm and face area.

4 Spread newspaper outdoors, lay the mermaid down, and spray her hair copper and her tail blue. Let everything dry, then peel off the pieces of vinyl.

5 Repeat steps 2 through 4 on the mermaid's back side.

6 Draw in a bikini top on your template, and use it as a guide for cutting out the copper mesh top. Attach it to the body with metal glue, and apply copper foil for straps.

7 Glue on the baubles. Add strings of pearls.

8 Bend and twist your mermaid into position. If needed, stabilize her with rocks or a vase of glass pebbles.

DESIGN TIP

To make the hand mirror, cut its shape out of the flashing. Mask the center with the adhesive vinyl. Spray paint the whole piece. When dry, remove the vinyl, revealing the shiny "mirror" in the center.

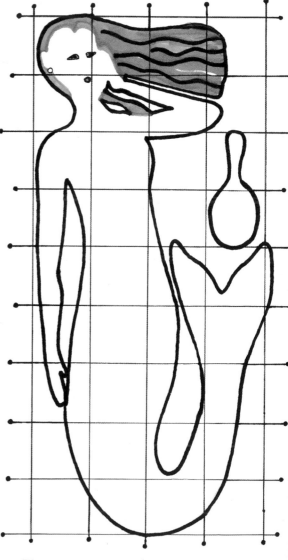

Figure 1: Mermaid & Mirror Template

Yard Guard

A welded warrior protects the farthest corners of your garden.
Rescued metal from autos and farm equipment make up his sturdy parts.

Design by
Jimmy Hopkins

INSTRUCTIONS

1 Trace your shoes or work boots onto the sheet metal. Freehand draw the toes and cut out the two feet with the torch. Put them aside to cool, then drill two ½ inch (1.3 cm) holes in the heel so you can spike the feet into the ground later.

2 For the legs, cut the 1½-inch (4 cm) diameter pipe into two equal sizes, approximately 3-½ feet (1.1 m) long. Put them aside.

3 Weld the muffler torso to the legs, keeping the legs spaced at the same angle. Turn the torso and legs over to prepare for adding the feet.

4 Place the feet flat on the welding table, putting left on left, right on right. Tack weld the legs onto the feet. Check your placement—if you're satisfied, weld it completely. The figure should now stand by itself.

5 Make the arm that holds the shield. Cut one of the 1-inch (2.5 cm) pipes to fit the shoulder—a 45° angle on one end and another 45° angle about 14 inches (35.5 cm) from the other end. Weld to the shoulder. Then form the elbow by cutting another piece of pipe off at 14 inches (35.5 cm), and welding it to the previously cut piece.

6 Add the shield by welding the disc onto the arm.

7 Repeat step 5 for the other arm, except when you weld on the last part of the arm, position it to hold the spear. Cut the solid metal rod off at 6 feet (1.8 m). Weld one end of it to one of the feet, and to the arm at the hand. Weld the finial to the top of the spear.

8 Form the neck by welding the 4-inch (10 cm) piece of pipe to the top center of the muffler. Position the plow piece as the head, and weld it in place. Add the washers for the eyes.

9 Make the spikes that will hold the guard upright. Cut the remaining 3 feet (.9 m) of the solid rod in half. Weld the remaining washers onto the end of each rod.

10 Drive the rods down through the holes in the feet into the ground.

DESIGN TIP

Once you start looking, you'll find terrific salvaged metal pieces everywhere.

I figured my guy might be a little lonely, so I made another welded warrior on the other side of the path. It's really funny to see them glaring at one another all day!
—Jimmy Hopkins

MATERIALS

METAL PIPES
* 1-inch (2.5 cm) dia., 6 feet (1.8 m) long, for arms and shoulders
* 1½-inch (4 cm) dia., 7 feet (2.1 m) long, for legs
* 4-inch (10 cm) dia., approx. 6 inches (15.2 cm) long, for neck

1 black marker
2 square feet (.6 m) of .125 sheet metal
½-inch (1.3 cm) dia. solid metal rod, 9 feet (2.7 m) long, for spear
Old muffler, for torso
Finial, for spear tip
Plow piece, for head
Harrow disc, for shield
2 washers, for eyes
2 washers, for feet spikes

TOOLS

Oxy/acetylene cutting torch
Welder
Metal cutting saw
Drill
½-inch (1.2 cm) drill bit

SAFETY GEAR

Safety glasses
Welding gloves and boots
Welding helmet
Leather apron

Plastic-Pot Couple

Design by John Buettner

Fritz and Betty are design winners from the North Carolina State Fair. The sweethearts share a secret—their skeletal structure is a simple pipe-within-a-pipe system—with connectors such as CDs and dinner plates! This internal system gives their plastic-pot bodies the rigidity they need to support the weight of flowers with potting soil and water. Clever painting gives them their rusty vintage look.

BEFORE YOU START

Items such as plastic pots and trashcans come in a variety of sizes while plastic and PVC plumbing pipe and connectors come in specific measurements. Plan the proportions of the statues around the pipes and connectors you find, not the containers.

Your local home improvement store is the source for most of the parts you'll need. Plastic or PVC pipes and connectors are found in the plumbing section; metal pipes and connectors are in the venting and heating supply sections.

Use the materials list and instructions as a general guide only, modifying them as desired.

INSTRUCTIONS

Preassembly

1 Based on the materials you have on hand, draw detailed sketches of your designs.

2 Measure and mark all the pieces.

3 Drill all the necessary holes in the containers and connector pieces; drill drainage holes in all the containers.

4 Because proper fit is crucial, assemble everything in a dry run before you glue the parts permanently. Use fig. 1 on page 96 to guide you.

DESIGN TIP

One-legged statues are far easier to make and more stable than the two-legged type because you're more likely to achieve a physically sound tower of containers with the weight being lined-up from the head to the ground. If your two-legged statue's torso starts leaning, straighten it up with small support wires from the shoulder to the outside edge of the large pelvis pot.

MATERIALS
for Both Two-Legged Fritz & One-Legged Betty

PLASTIC OR PVC PIPE

1 3-inch (7.6 cm) dia. pipe, 10 feet (3 m) long, cut as follows:

* 3 pieces, each 24 inches (61 cm) long, for legs (the length should be in proportion to your pots) (#1)

1 1¼-inch (3.2 cm) dia. pipe, 10 feet (3 m) long, cut as follows:

* 2 pieces, each 17½ inches (44.5 cm) long, for torsos (#2)
* 2 pieces, each 3 inches (7.6 cm) long, for necks (#3)
* 4 pieces, each 5 inches (12.7 cm) long, for wrists (#4)

2 1-inch (2.5 cm) dia. pipe, 10 feet (3 m) long, cut as follows:

* 4 pieces, each 10 inches (10.2 cm) long, for forearms (#6)
* 2 pieces, each 11 inches (17.9 cm) long, for torsos (#7)
* 4 pieces, each 4 inches (10.2 cm) long, for shoulders (#8)
* 2 scrap pieces, each 1 inch (2.5 cm) long, for neck details (#9)

2 plastic 4-way connectors, 1-inch (2.5 cm) dia., used as central connector (#10)
8 plastic elbows, 40° or 45°, 1-inch (2.5 cm) dia., for arms (#11) and shoulders (#12)
3 household plumbing closet flanges (marked 3 x 4 on box), used as leg/pelvic connectors (#13)
2 plastic test caps, used as neck/head washers (#14)

continued on next page

MATERIALS
for Both Two-Legged Fritz & One-Legged Betty *continued*

PLASTIC GARDEN POTS & KITCHENWARE
* 2 "tall" pots approx. 8¼ inches (21 cm) high, for heads (#15)
* 2 smaller pots to take up space inside the heads (#16)
* 2 basin pots approx. 18 inches (45.7) wide, for pelvises (#17)
* 1 thin-walled pot, to be cut up for Betty's decorations (#18)
* 2 plastic trashcans approx. 12 inches tall (30.5 cm), for torsos (#19)
* 2 plastic dinner plates, 9-inch (22.9 cm) dia., used as washers (#20) inside the pelvis pots

METAL PIPES & CONNECTORS
* 2 threaded pipes ¾-inch (1.9 cm) dia., 10 inches (25.4 cm) long, used as pelvis-to-torso support (#21)
* 2 pipe nipples, ¾-inch (1.9 cm) dia., 3½ inches (8.9 cm) long, used as neck support (#22)
* 4 metal floor flanges to fit the threaded pipes, used as pot-to-pipe connectors (#23)
* 1 metal vent junction cap, to decorate Fritz's head (#24)

2 cork disks, used as washers (#25) inside pelvis pots
2 CDs, used as washers (#26) outside head pots
16 bolts, 3 inches (7.6 cm) long, with matching washers and nuts
Assortment of small screws, washers, nuts, and bolts
Tube of glue that bonds plastic and metal
Can of PVC glue
Assortment of small-and medium-gauge wire
2 pairs of nonporous (plastic, rubber or vinyl) gloves
Plastic utensils & toys
4 plastic practice golf balls, for eyes
Wire mesh, as desired
2 pinecones
3 metal or wood fence posts, taller than the leg pipes
Flat black spray paint
Orange spray paint
Small tube of dark brown acrylic paint
Small tube of medium purple acrylic paint

TOOLS
Handsaw
Power drill with variety of drill bits including 1-inch (2.5 cm) and 2-inch (5 cm) holesaw bits
Hot-glue gun with plenty of hot-glue sticks
Screwdrivers, pliers, wirecutters as needed
Sponges or rags

Make the Body Parts

5 Make one figure at a time, starting with the head. Predrill holes in all the head pieces to match the holes in the metal floor flange (#23). Assemble the pieces with the bolts threaded upwards through: the flange, the CD (#25, used as a washer), the bottom of the head pot (#15), and the test cap (#14, used as a washer). Use small nuts to tighten the bolts—don't overtighten as this could crack the support pieces.

6 Screw the top of the metal pipe nipple (#22) into the flange. Set the neck/head unit aside.

7 Repeat steps 5 and 6 for the other figure.

Make Betty's One-Legged Lower Body

8 Drill holes and line up the pieces for the pelvis and leg. With the bonding glue, attach the cork disk (#25) to the bottom of the pelvis pot (#17), making it level. Then snugly glue the closet flange (#13) to the disc. For the top side of the pot, drill and screw into place the metal floor flange (#23) face side up onto the upside down plastic dinner plate (#20). Thread the bolts face up, so that the nuts don't interfere with the snug fit needed between the plate and the pot surface. Then use the bonding glue to attach the plate/flange unit onto the inside bottom of the pot. After the glue has dried, drill holes through the entire pelvic structure, and secure with bolts, washers and nuts. Again, don't overtighten.

9 Slide the leg pipe (#1) up into the closet flange (#13) beneath the pot and apply the bonding glue. Or, if you're planning to move the figure, just leave the leg unglued; it fits snugly into the flange.

10 Screw the bottom end of the metal pelvis-to torso support pipe (#21) into the metal flange (#23) inside the pelvis pot.

Make Fritz's Two-Legged Lower Body

11 Follow steps 8 to 10, except do it for two legs—simply trim the two remaining closet flanges (#17) to fit side by side under the pelvis pot.

Make the Torsos

12 With the large holesaw bit, bore two holes in the front of the trashcan torso (#19) for Betty's breasts.

13 With the same bit, bore a hole at least 1-¼-inch (3.2 cm) wide through the trashcan bottom for the pipe structure. Use the smaller holesaw bit to make armholes on the side of the torso. (See fig. 1.)

18 Repeat steps 13 to 17 for Fritz.

Connect the Head & Neck

19 Wrap the small piece of scrap plastic pipe (#9) around the threaded bottom end of the pipe nipple (#22) to extend the neck about ¾ inch (1.9 cm) and allow it to fit tightly into the connector (#10). Before making this connection, slide the neck section (#3) into place over the nipple (#22). Insert the exposed tip into the connector, and fuse it with the PVC glue.

Make the Hands

20 Make hand and finger shapes out of the heavy wire, inset them into the gloves, then stuff each finger carefully with plastic grocery bags. Attach the hands to the wrist pipes (#4) with small screws or wire, then glue the wrist pipes onto the arms.

14 Make the layered 3-pipe support section. Wedge the smallest diameter plastic torso support pipe (#7) onto the threaded end of the metal pelvis-to-torso support pipe (#21), making a snug fit. Then slide the wider-diameter plastic torso pipe (#2) over the two combined pipes, so that at least ¾ inch (1.9 cm) of the central metal pipe (#21) extends out the top.

15 Place the trashcan into position over the combined pipes, then glue the bottom of 4-way connector (#10) onto the protruding tip of the torso support pipe (#7). When you are satisfied that the pieces all fit snugly, fuse the pipes together with the PVC glue, which will seep into all the pipes and seal them permanently.

16 It's a little tricky to access the connector (#10) inside the trash can, so glue the left shoulder piece (#8) into the left side of the connector (#10), position the torso/trashcan, and then use the PVC glue to attach the other shoulder (#8). Leave the top of the connector open for now.

17 Position and glue the arms (#5 and #6) and the elbows (# 11 and #12) with the PVC glue. If you want arms that you can reposition, drill holes and screw them together instead of gluing them.

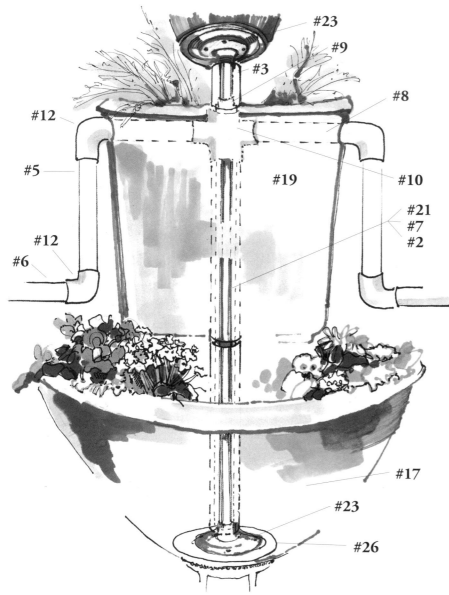

Figure 1: Internal Structure

Add Decorations

21 Now the fun begins! Use any type of plastic bonding glue or hot glue and a glue gun to secure various decorative elements, such as small plastic utensils or toys. (See the photo.) Make noses and Betty's headdress out of pieces from the thin-walled pot (#18). Make eyes from plastic practice golf balls. Use wire or wire mesh to make bow ties and lacy trim. Make Fritz's crown from the metal vent junction cap (#24). Add Betty's pinecone breasts. Use the hot glue to draw on facial features and inscribe details onto the pots and pipes.

Install the Fence Posts

22 Insert the metal fence posts into the ground far enough so that the legs can fit over them. Tape sections of scrap plastic pipes to the posts to improve their fit if needed. Slip the legs over the posts.

Paint the Figures

23 Prime all the statue surfaces with black spray paint to help the other paints adhere and even out the overall color.

24 To create a rusty appearance, use a paint kit purchased from a home supply store. Or make your own mixture as I did. Apply a base coat of pumpkin orange enamel spray to the entire surface. Let dry. (Plastic can sometimes repel paint; if your paint doesn't stick to the plastic, rub the area with paint thinner before you finish painting.) Use a sponge or rag to dab on a watered-down mix of the purple and brown acrylic paints. Experiment in small areas with different amounts of stains until you get the most authentic rusted metal look.

Add Flowers

25 Turn the smaller pots (#16) upside down in the head pot to take up space and plant the flowers. Add potting soil and flowers to the pelvis pot.

An elephant's trunk is made from the leg of a potbelly stove.

Like many outdoor figure designers, metal artist Jimmy Hopkins prefers to work with salvaged materials, particularly salvaged metal. Coming from small-town Georgia, he's able to find many old pieces of farm equipment and other cast-off machinery that he turns into delightful sculptures that look even more garden-friendly after they've acquired a rusty patina. ALL PHOTOS BY SANDRA STAMBAUGH

Garden tools make some of the prettiest yard birds.

Salvaged metal makes pigs that march in formation-and fly!

A shovel turns this bird into a bird feeder.

Design by Merry Miller

MATERIALS
FABRIC
* 3 yards (2.7 m) natural burlap
* 2 yards (1.8 m) burlap, dyed with natural dyes
* 1 sq. yard (.9 sq. m) heavy upholstery fabric

2 2 x 2s, 8 feet (2.4 m) long (see Cutting List below)
Wood screws, as needed
4 corner braces, 1½ x ½ inches (3.8 x 1.3 cm)
¾-inch (1.9 cm) plywood, 2 feet (61 cm) square
Wood stain
20-gauge galvanized steel wire
Twine
Nails
Hardware cloth as needed
Rebar, ½-inch (1.3 cm) dia., 6 feet (1.8 m) long

BIRD FOOD
* Metal suet feeding basket (found in bird supply stores)
* Birdseed
* Millet wands (optional)

CUTTING LIST: 2 x 2s
1 piece, 6 feet (1.8 m) long, for spine
1 piece, 20 inches (50.8 cm) long, for shoulder
1 piece, 2 feet (61 cm) long, for hips
2 pieces, 11 inches (27.9 cm) long, for upper arm
2 pieces, 14 inches (35.6 cm) long, for lower arm

TOOLS
Handsaw
Drill
Countersink drill bit
Screwdriver
Jigsaw
Stapler
Scissors
Wire cutters
Hammer

Medieval Maid Birdfeeder

A disciple of St. Francis steps out of the medieval forest to give herself to the birds. She offers food to them from her tray and the decorations in her hair and clothes. In spring, the birds pull threads of her burlap gown to make safe nesting material.

INSTRUCTIONS

1 As in fig. 1 on page 101, drill and screw the three body pieces together. To create different levels on which to hang the cloth—place the shoulder about 14 inches (35.6 cm) from the top front of the spine; the hip piece about 30 inches (76.2 cm) on the back.

2 Secure the arm pieces together in a right angle with the corner braces. Then screw the arms to the front of the shoulder piece.

3 Make the head/neck piece by drawing on the plywood a 10-inch-wide (25.4-cm) oval with a 4-inch-long (10.2 cm) long neck rectangle. Cut with the jigsaw and set aside.

4 If you want to make the birdseed storage box (see Design Tip on page 101), do it now.

5 Stain the figure's head and body parts now. Paint on a face if you wish. Let dry.

6 Staple layered strips of burlap to the top and back of the head, with a few shorter strips in the front. Thread wire through the strip centers, loop them, and pinch. Voila! You've got a few curls to withstand even the severest weather.

7 Make the lady's garments, but don't attach her head yet. Form the under-tunic from the upholstery fabric. Fold the fabric in half horizontally, cut on the fold and in the center to make a small semicircle, slip it over the spine, and let the fabric droop over the shoulder in a natural fold. (See fig. 2 on page 100.)

8 From the colored burlap, cut another tunic shape, longer but narrower than the first one, with a slit in the front make an open neckline.

9 Double the length of the figure from bottom to shoulder board, and cut a piece of natural burlap twice that length. Use the burlap as it comes from the bolt, and then fold, gather, or trim as you like. As you did previously, fold and cut a center neckhole, then slip the gown over the other two garments. Pull up the colored burlap to make a collar in a contrasting color. Make sure the large sleeves of the upholstery undertunic are still visible.

10 The upholstery fabric undertunic on either side of the shoulder board will have naturally collapsed into folds, from which you can make pockets to hold small bags of birdseed. Hold the pieces of the folds together while you use the twine to sew big visible stitches in the shape of a semicircle. (See fig. 2. below.) With scrap burlap, make two little bags to fit into the pockets. Pin them onto the tunic, and stuff them with seed, or insert floral foam and stick in wands of millet as the designer did.

Figure 2: Medieval Maid Birdfeeder Tunic with Pockets

11 Make straps of braided raffia on either side of the metal suet feeding basket and attach to the hip bar underneath the tunic.

12 The three-sided bird feeder rests snugly on top of and between the figure's arms, open in the back, so you can easily remove it to add more seed and clean it. Cut the bottom of the tray: the length of the distance between the outstretched forearms from outside edge to outside edge, plus ½ inch (1.3 cm); the width is the distance from the inside of the elbow to the end of the forearms, plus ½ inch. The sides are each 3 inches (7.6 cm) high and their lengths are ½ inch longer than the length and width of the bottom sides. Cut scalloped tops to make roosting spots. Use finishing nails to nail the side pieces flush to the bottom. Drill small drainage holes. Drill holes along the sides and insert small dowels as bird perches. If you want to stain the wood, do it now and let dry.

13 Drill and screw the head/neck unit to the front of the spine, about ½ inch (1.3 cm) above the shoulder to give it enough room to tilt a bit.

14 Drive the rebar into the ground, and attach the lady with wire or rope.

DESIGN TIP

Make a small rectangular seed storage box for the back of her head. Drill drainage holes. Attach the box with nails pounded in from the front of the head. Cover the top with hardware cloth, which small birds can roost on while they peck the lady's hair. Staple it at one end to allow easy access to the birdseed inside.

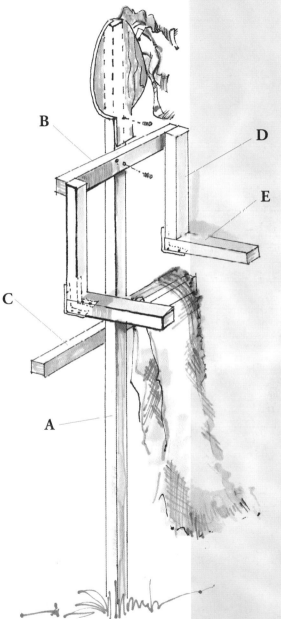

Figure 1: Medieval Maid Birdfeeder Frame

Moss Angel

Grace your garden with a living angel, adorned with moss and lichen, sharing a basket of fresh flowers.

BEFORE YOU START

1 It's ideal to make the angel where you intend to keep her. If you must construct her somewhere else, place her in a big empty pot, setting the plant supports on the pot's rim with their stakes in empty space. Using protective gloves, carry the completed angel from its bottom.

2 For the best color, use fresh plant material. Shake off the dirt, trimming it with scissors if necessary, to reduce the amount of moist surface to be glued.

INSTRUCTIONS

1 Put together the plant support armature, starting at the bottom and working up. Make the round gown base by attaching the two large wire semicircles at the bottom. (Refer to fig. 1 on page 104 throughout.) About 13 inches (33 cm) from the top, place the 9-inch (23 cm) circle that helps make the shoulders and support the hanging basket.

2 To build the angel's gown, first cut hardware cloth to the same circumference as the base and as wide as you can comfortably work. (The designer used pieces 12 to 14 inches [30.5 to 35.6 cm] wide.) Both poultry netting and hardware cloth are easily malleable, but the curl of the metal as it comes off the roll can be dangerously sharp. Working in narrow strips, and building the dress in small pieces like a patchwork quilt, is more time-consuming but safer.

3 Press and fold the hardware cloth into the skirt's upside-down cone shape. Add strips of poultry netting to the hardware cloth by twisting its loose wires through the holes of the hardware cloth. Continue in the same manner until you finish the skirt.

4 Make the bodice from a tube of netting about 2 ½ feet x 16 inches (76 x 40.6 cm), with both ends attached. Slide the tube a little bit over the top of the cone, and attach by twisting the loose wires. Press and fold the poultry netting in at the sides to shape the bodice.

5 Make the shoulders. Cut a piece of hardware cloth to cover the open end of her bodice. Before wiring the pieces together, make certain that the 9-inch (23 cm) circular support fits into the bodice top and that the hardware cloth is resting on the support.

6 Make the neck from a tube of netting about 14 x 7 inches (35.6 x 17.8 cm). Attach to the shoulders, making certain that the vertical stem of the main plant support is at the back of the tube neck—the angel's neck must be strong and securely attached to the main support.

7 Hang the basket over the neck, and affix it with wire to the bodice.

8 Make the arms with a tube of netting 14 feet (4.2 m) wide that measures from the right shoulder to the center of the basket and back around to the left shoulder. Attach one end to each shoulder, making certain that it embraces the basket.

9 Make the head by folding and pressing a 14-inch (35.6 cm) square of poultry netting into an egg shape and attaching it to the neck. The head should be about 8 inches (20.3 cm) high.

Angel Design
by Merry Miller
Nature Design
by Cynthia Gillooly

MATERIALS

2 half-circle plant supports, 21-inch (53 cm) dia.
1 full-circle plant support, 9-inch (23 cm) dia.
Hardware cloth
Poultry netting with 1-inch (2.5 cm) hexagons
5-foot-long (1.5 m) plastic plant support with connectors, capable of adding additional circular supports (found in garden stores)
Hanging basket with a chain and moss-covered bowl
20-gauge spool wire for weaving the netting
Hot-glue gun and glue sticks
Moss of various colors and textures
Lichen
Pinecones of various sizes
Seasonal flowers
Potting soil
2 rattan-vine wall decorations, size and shape of wings

TOOLS

Wire cutters
Tin snips
Measuring tape

10 Apply sections of moss from the base of the angel upward, using the thickest moss on the skirt and the thinner moss on the arms and head. Use gobs of hot—not cool—glue, and press each moss section firmly against the poultry netting frame for about 15 to 20 seconds to make sure as much glue as possible connects. Apply lichen and pinecones as appropriate.

11 Place an arrangement of seasonal flowers in the angel's basket, filling it with enough potting soil to keep it moist. Water it gently as needed. Gently spray the entire figure with water to keep the moss fresh-looking longer.

12 Add the wings, wiring the fans to the back of the angel's shoulders. You can also make wings out of poultry netting, bolstered by the hardware cloth.

DESIGN TIP

Place the angel in a shady spot of the garden where visitors can sit with her and contemplate nature's beauty.

Figure 1: Moss Angel

Notice the incredible detail sculptor Dave Rogers puts into this spider portrait.

New York sculptor Dave Rogers is world famous for his unique yard figures—dinosaur-sized bugs! Each one is meticulously carved from wood and other natural materials. When not decorating his yard, the insects go on exhibit at botanical gardens, thrilling bug lovers of all ages. ALL PHOTOS COURTESY OF THE ARTIST, PHOTOS BY HARRY GROD.

Ladybug, carved from red cedar, can't fly away home very quickly— she weighs 25 pounds (11 kg).

Earwig, carved from red cedar, is more than 7 feet (2.1m) long.

Gazing-Ball Scarecrow

There's no such thing as an ordinary corn patch if it's guarded by a scarecrow with a gazing ball head blazing in the sun.

Design by
Christi and
Simon Whiteley

INSTRUCTIONS

1. Lay the porch post and corbels on the ground. Measure and mark 3 inches (7.6 cm) down from the top of the post on the two opposite sides. Using the nail gun, attach the corbels evenly to the post below the marks. (If you don't have a nail gun, use the power drill to predrill holes before you drive the nails. Old wood is so dense that if you don't take such precautions, you could split it.)

2. With the 1-inch (2.5 cm) screws, attach each L-bracket to the post where it meets the corbel.

3. Dig a posthole and insert the figure. See page 17 for information on posthole digging.

4. After the post is stabilized, place the neck of the gazing ball into the top of the post.

"Simplicity..."
—Christi Whiteley

DESIGN TIP

There are so many gazing balls on the market today—you'd have no trouble making a scarecrow with a colorful mosaic ball, or one with a pearly moonlight glow.

MATERIALS

Porch post with hollow center, about 6 feet (1.8 m) in height, for the body

2 large corbels for the arms

Gazing ball (new or old) for the head

2 2-inch-long (5 cm) L-brackets

TOOLS

Tape measure

Nail gun with 3-inch-long (7.6 cm) finish nails or power drill

1-inch-long (2.5 cm) wood screws

Design by Joan K. Morris

Harvest Sweethearts

Their arms joined happily, Bobby Joe and his high-kickin' Patty Sue do their fancy dancing side by side. Stuff them with straw and quilt batting for a traditional, yet smooth, look.

MATERIALS

4 1 x 2s, 8 feet (2.4 m) long (see Cutting List below)

20 1½-inch-long (3.8 cm) wood screws

Scraps of muslin large enough to make 2 heads and 2 hands

Hair-colored yarn

Quilt batting

1 12-inch (30.5 cm) square of brown felt

Straw for stuffing

2 old small bed pillows

Man's clothes, including shoes and socks

Woman's clothes, including shoes and socks

2 4-foot-long (1.2 m) rebars

2 4-inch-long (10.2 cm)repair strips

TOOLS

Jigsaw or handsaw

Pencil

Measuring tape

Phillips-head screwdriver

Scissors

Needle and thread

Yarn needle

Staple gun and staples

Safety pins

White glue

Drill

CUTTING LIST: 1 x 2s

2 pieces, 7 feet (2.1 m) long, for each spine (A)

1 piece, 31 inches (78.7 cm) long, for man's arm/shoulder (B)

1 piece, 23 inches (58.4 cm)long, woman's arm/shoulder (C)

2 pieces, 15 inches (38.4 cm)long, for upper legs for both (D)

1 piece, 18 inches (45.7 cm)long, for woman's outside arm (E)

2 pieces, 12 inches (30.5 cm)long, for lower legs for both (F)

INSTRUCTIONS

1 Assemble the scarecrows on the ground, and screw the pieces in place as indicated in fig. 1 on page 111.

2 From the muslin, cut two head-shaped pieces for each figure. Stitch around the edges, leaving the neck open. Turn right side out.

3 Stitch long pieces of yarn to the top of the woman's head to make hair. Cut to length as you like.

4 From the muslin, cut out two nose shapes, stuff them with a little quilt batting, and sew them on the face.

5 Cut the facial features from the felt, and glue on.

6 Stuff the heads, pull them over the spines to where they meet the shoulder pieces, tying the loose ends together, or stitching them closed. Staple them to the shoulder pieces.

7 If you have pillows, make the man's belly by stapling the pillows onto the shoulder piece, and letting them hang down.

"It's astonishing how characters come alive as you dress them and add accessories." — Joan K. Morris

8 For each figure, cut pieces of the quilt batting to wrap around the arms, legs, and torso. Staple in place.

9 Dress the figures, starting with the under layer of clothes and working your way out. Use safety pins or hand stitches to hold things in place. Slip spines down each character's inside leg. Shape the woman's legs with pantyhose. Position the shoes, predrill, and screw them into place.

10 Stuff the socks with straw, and squeeze them into the shoes.

11 Push the tops of the socks under the man's pant legs and over the woman's nylon stockings, leaving some straw hanging out.

12 On the muslin, trace your hands, cut four hand shapes, and sew two together for each hand, leaving the wrist open. Stuff the hands, and staple them in place, leaving some straw hanging out.

13 Stitch or glue on the man's hat.

14 Screw a repair strip to each side of the inside arms.

15 Add rebar to the spines, and insert the figures into the ground. When the figures are placed properly, screw the repair strips together to join the figures.

DESIGN TIP

Since the figures can be separated just by unscrewing the repair strips, you can easily change the couple's outfits.

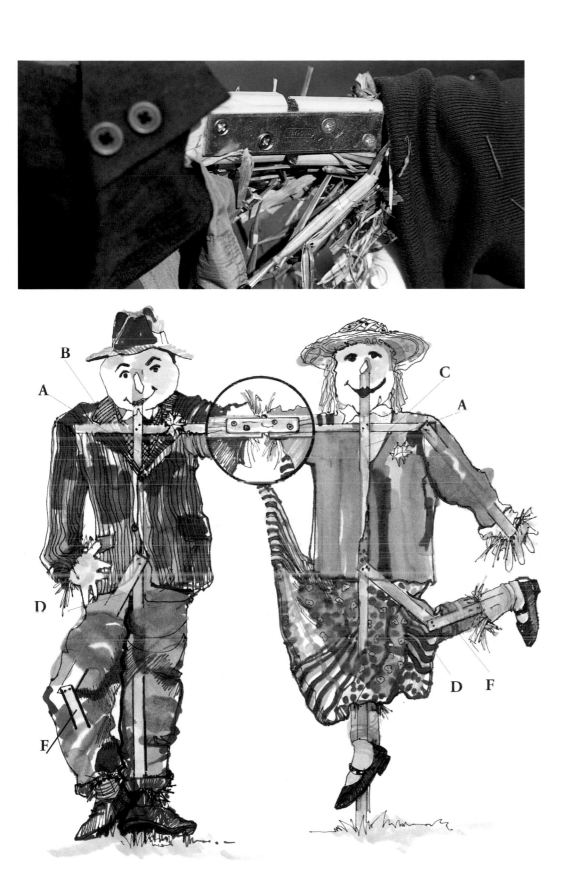

Figure 1: Harvest Sweethearts Frames & Connection

Design by
Terry Taylor

Trojan Tin Man

Inspired by Trojan War imagery, this modern tin man carries himself with the bearing of an ancient warrior. Held together with simple tack soldering, he'll rust gracefully for several seasons.

MATERIALS

Steel cans (not aluminum) in a variety of sizes and shapes
Magnet
Flat, metal pan for a base, such as an oil pan
Abrasive pads
Cookie sheet
Scrap tin or metal flashing
Paint for face (optional)

TOOLS

File
Awl
Pop rivet tool and rivets
Tin snips
Propane torch, solder, and flux (found with plumbing supplies)

"Soldering is an excellent way to make metal yard figures without having to weld—especially during the winter, when making garden projects can chase away the winter blues."
— Terry Taylor

BEFORE YOU START

1 Gather a variety of cans. Make sure the cans and your flat pan are made of steel and not aluminum, because you can't solder aluminum. If a magnet sticks to a can, it's steel based. Use gallon-sized cans for the torso, large juice cans for the legs, and various other sizes for the rest of the man.

2 Remove one end of each can. Wash and dry the cans thoroughly. (This is important especially if you aren't going to create the tin man right away. Otherwise, you'll wind up with a stash of smelly cans.) Use the file to smooth any jagged edges on the interior rims of the cans.

INSTRUCTIONS

1 Arrange the cans on a flat surface. Notice that the sizes of the cans vary, giving the man a lively appearance that isn't achieved when the cans are all the same size. Make a rough sketch of their placement. Number the cans with sticky notes if you wish.

2 Pierce drainage holes with the awl in the end of each can to prevent the cans from filling with water.

3 Use the pop rivet tool and rivets to join pairs of large cans together for the torso. Align the pairs, mark a place on each can, and pierce the marks with the awl. Cut four strips of metal (the size doesn't really matter), and pierce holes in each end. Rivet the straps to the cans to join the parts of the torso.

4 With an abrasive pad, scour the rims and bottoms of cans that will form the arms and legs. Flux and solder the cans together one at a time. A cookie sheet is a good, inexpensive work surface. Clean the solder joints with soap and water after you've soldered them, and set them aside.

5 Cut simple hand shapes out of scrap tin or flashing. Rivet each one to an arm.

6 Make the head and neck by soldering the gallon-size can to a smaller can. Make a nose out of a triangle of scrap tin. Cut off the top point of the triangle with your shears. Score the metal with the awl, and bend the sides to shape them. Solder on the nose.

7 Solder the legs to the assembled torso.

8 Solder the legs and torso to the flat pan base.

9 Pierce a hole in each "shoulder" of the torso. Pierce a hole in the side of each arm. Rivet the arms to the shoulders.

10 Solder the neck to the rims of the upper torso. This is a bit of a balancing act since you're soldering in only four small places, but it's not hard to accomplish.

DESIGN TIP

You can usually get large-sized cans from local restaurants and school cafeterias. You'll get a positive response if you offer to come get them on a specified date and time.

Backyard Totem Pole

Carved out of full-grown cedar trees by the native people of the Pacific Northwest, totem poles symbolized the history of individual families or clans. Create a backyard version from a porch post and playfully colored paints.

BEFORE YOU START

Many beautiful books illustrate West Coast Indian art and the symbolism of carved figures. Since it's your totem pole, animals and other carvings can symbolize whatever you'd like them to.

INSTRUCTIONS

1 Using the factory-designed sections on your post, determine the general placement of each figure.

2 Wearing protective gloves and safety glasses, carve the figures on the pole. Use the rotary tool fitted with the round wood-carving bit to outline each figure. Then, with the rotary tool or hand tools, carve as much as you like.

3 With the jigsaw, cut two pieces of 1 x 6 into 12-inch (30.5 cm) lengths. Draw the shape of the wings onto each piece. Outline the shape of the feathers with the rotary tool.

4 Draw beak shapes on two small pieces of wood, and carve the outline of the mouth.

5 Screw the wings and beaks to the post.

6 Sand the post and bird top, and wipe clean.

7 Stain the post. Spread a mixture of 50:50 brown paint and glaze on the post. Use the rag to wipe it into all the spaces. Save some of the mixture.

8 Paint the animals and other figures inside the lines and let dry. Blacken the lines around the figures with the liner brush and paint. Let dry.

9 Add another coat of glaze to all the painted figures. Wipe off immediately and let dry.

10 Spray the whole post with three or more coats of polyurethane spray, letting it dry thoroughly between coats.

11 Dig a posthole and insert the post. See page 17 for instructions.

"My totem pole symbolizes a friend's family—the eagle is the father; owl is mother; wolf is the oldest son, frog is the daughter; raccoon is the youngest son. The family dog is the low man on the pole— a place of honor holding up the rest of the family. Houses dedicate the pole as a house-warming present."
—Joan K. Morris

Design by Joan K. Morris

MATERIALS

WOOD
* Porch post, 8 feet (2.4 m) tall, salvaged or new from a home supply store
* 1 x 6, 2 feet (.6 m) long, for wings
* 2 pieces of scrap wood, about 1 x 3 x 5 inches (2.5 x 7.6 x 12.7 cm)

10 2-inch-long (5 cm) wood screws
Wood paint, your choice of colors, and black
Water-based glaze
Spray polyurethane

TOOLS

Pencil
Rotary tool and wood carving bits
Wood carving tools (small kit from craft store)
Jigsaw
Drill
Screwdriver
Sandpaper
Paintbrushes, 1 inch (2.5 cm) and 2 inch (5 cm) and thin liner
Rags
Posthole digger

SAFETY GEAR

Protective gloves
Safety glasses

Neighborhood Watch

By creating good-humored frontyard vignettes, you can inspire neighbors to get together on community issues. A roller skater, a flowerbox gardener, a black cat, and a happy bluebird keep watchful eyes on the neighborhood.

INSTRUCTIONS

1 Measure and cut shelving board to make the four sides of the flowerbox, and nail or screw them together. Prime and paint. When dry, staple a cut piece of hardware cloth to the bottom, from outer edge to edge. Cut four legs of an appropriate height for the figures, such as the 29-inch legs (73.6 cm) in the photo. Prime and spray the legs and when dry, nail or screw them to the flower box. For better stability, attach four sturdy corner braces.

2 Make the rectangular window from canvas stretcher frames that already have mitered corners. Prime and paint. Screw one of the shorter sides of the frame to the back of the flowerbox. Make the structure wind-proof by tacking two 1 x 2s on the back from the top of the side window frames down the flowerbox legs. Paint to match.

3 Draw the figures' heads on the plywood, and cut them out with a jigsaw. Set aside.

4 Make the figures from sections of the 1 x 2s, cut and assembled to your design. The more moveable parts you have with figures, as in the figures' arms, the more gestures you can achieve. Using screws instead of nails allows you to create funny tilts and exaggerated poses. The flowerbox gardener has little flowerpots as hair, requiring sturdy support. For her shoulder, use a 2 x 2, and screw her head in front of the shoulder.

5 Attach the heads to their bodies. Prime and paint.

6 Dress your characters. Notice the special touches that reveal the personality of the characters, such as eyeglasses and footwear.

7 Predrill guide holes with a nail or awl, then screw small clay pots onto the flowerbox gardener's head. Stuff the pots with floral foam, and insert lively posies. With cup hooks or screw eyes add colored whistles to the skater's skirt. Fill the flowerbox with flowerpots. Add pets, such as the cat and the bluebird.

"I created this design so I could make fun of my older sister, and now she won't give me my skates back!"
—*Merry Miller*

Design by Merry Miller

MATERIALS
for Two Figures

WOOD
* Pine shelving board, 8 feet (2.4 m) long, for flower box
* 2 pieces of 2 x 2, 8 feet (2.4 m) long, for flower box legs
* 3 pieces of 1 x 2, 8 feet (2.4 m) long, for window support
* 2 pairs of canvas stretcher bars, 28 inches (71 cm) and 36 inches (91.4 cm) long, to make the window frame
* ¾-inch (1.9 cm) plywood, 2 feet square (61 cm)

Wood screws or nails
Spray primer paint
Spray enamel, your choice of colors
Small roll of hardware cloth
4 corner braces
Colorful clothing for two characters
Colorful accessories
Tiny flower pots and silk posies
Floral foam

TOOLS

Measuring tape
Saw
Hammer
Screwdriver
Drill with countersink bit
Staple gun
Jigsaw
Awl

Birchwood Family Banquet

Have the whole family help prepare this banquet. You cut the wood pieces, and let the youngsters assemble them. It might take all summer to make—but my, oh my, on that first day of snow, it will be a sight to remember!

INSTRUCTIONS

1 Decide how many figures you want and their size. Using fig. 1 to guide you, design the parts on graph paper. Calculate how much wood you'll need. Birch is ideal for this project because its bark is so beautiful, but you can use any available wood.

2 Set aside nine containers or sorting areas for each section of wood: hat, head, neck, torso, upper arms, forearms, thighs, lower legs, and noses. Cut all the pieces according to your design.

3 Assemble one or two figures yourself so you can solve any problems ahead of time.

4 Use the photo to make the table accessories, such as the loaves of bread, the plates, and the centerpieces.

5 On the day (s) you assemble the figures, set out containers of nails, appropriate to your figures' dimensions, and have enough hammers on hand for everyone.

6 Let the older children nail the pieces together; have the younger children glue on the noses and eyes. While the project looks awesomely elegant with so many figures with similar faces, it can be charming with different faces painted and put together by the children.

7 Set the figures securely on the benches. Decorate the table with the accessories.

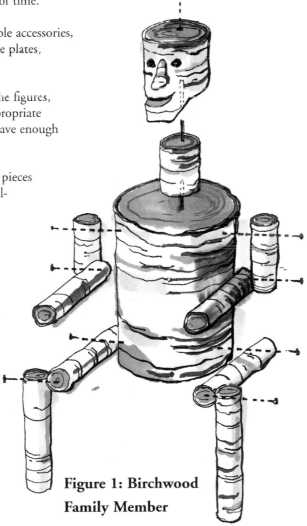

Figure 1: Birchwood Family Member

MATERIALS
for One Figure

TREE SECTIONS
* 1 firm section of a tree trunk, for the body
* 1 section of a tree trunk, narrower than the body, for the head
* 1 section of a tree trunk, wider than the body, for the hat
* 1 short branch, narrower than the head, for the neck
* 8 branches to cut to size for arms and legs
* 1 scrap piece for the nose

Nails or wood screws of appropriate sizes to attach all the pieces
Wood glue
Black cabochons for eyes

TOOLS

Power saw
Hand saw
Power drill
Hammer

The Flake Out Festival in Wisconsin Dells, Wisconsin, is a chance for local sculptors to do their thing. Experts say the best temperature for snow sculpting is 20°F (6.6°C) above 0.

PHOTO COURTESY WISCONSIN DELLS VISITOR & CONVENTION BUREAU, BY SCOTT WITTE

Folks in Valdez, Alaska, get pretty tired of seeing white, so they add summer colors to their snow figures. Spray paint makes the brightest hues; pale colors come from colored sugar drinks.

PHOTOS COURTESY LAURIE PRAX, VALDEZ, ALASKA

Don't let winter put a stop to yard figures! Natural ingredients make the loveliest decorations for snow people.

120

This giant figure is made from cast-off pieces of wood. It will probably be dismantled when the festival is over. PHOTO COURTESY OF SOCIETÉ DE L'EPOUVANTAIL, DENENS, SWITZERLAND

Only two natural ingredients—tree logs and pinecones—are used in this majestic figure. PHOTO COURTESY OF SOCIETÉ DE L'EPOUVANTAIL, DENENS, SWITZERLAND

This figure, made from old barnwood and wire, is now a valued piece in an American art lover's collection. PHOTO COURTESY JOHN FOSTER, ENVISION FOLK ART OF MISSOURI

Design by
Dyan Mai Peterson

Gourd Gardenkeeper

Though he wears war paint to scare off avian invaders,
this artfully decorated gourd is more friendly than fierce.

MATERIALS

GOURDS AND GOURD PARTS

* Canteen gourd, medium size, cleaned, for the head
* Section cut from the neck of a martin gourd, for the neck
* 2 round slices cut from a dipper gourd, for the eyes
* 6 ornamental gourds, cleaned, to hang from the arms
* Gourd vine and tendrils, for hair and neck

2 1 x 3s, cut to 60 inches (52 cm) long each, for spine and arms
18-gauge wire, about 8 feet (2.43 m) in length
6-inch-long (2.5 cm) nails
Leather dyes: British tan, black, mahogany
Quick-set epoxy glue
Brown waxed linen thread
Spar varnish (optional)

TOOLS

Stiff scrubbing brush
Pencil
Pyrography tool with a straight-line burning tip
Handheld hair dryer
Handsaw
Jigsaw
1-inch (2.5 cm) foam brush
Cotton swabs
Scissors

SAFETY GEAR

Dust mask or respirator

INSTRUCTIONS

1 Clean the gourds outside. Use warm water and a stiff brush to remove any dirt and mold. Be careful not to scratch the surface. Allow to dry. Wear protective mask or respirator when working with gourds.

2 Draw the face lines on the gourd.

3 Use the pyrography tool with the straight-line burning tip to burn in all the lines.

4 With the foam brush, apply the leather dyes to color portions of the face. Dye the mouth, leaving the top portion natural. Use cotton swabs to color in small areas. Dry the face and eyes with the hair dryer. Glue on the gourd eyes.

5 To create hair, bundle gourd stems with tendrils attached in different sizes and lengths. Wrap the waxed linen thread around the center of the bundle several times, tying a double knot to hold it. Glue the hair in place and set the head aside to dry.

6 To make the arms, cut the ends of one 1 x 3 at an angle. Cross the arm board and the spine and nail or screw where they intersect. Leave 6 inches (15.2 cm) at the top of the spine so you can fit it inside the gourd head.

7 Hammer nails on both sides of the arms, and attach the ornamental gourds with wire. Leave extra wire at both ends, and wrap it around a pencil to create a tendril effect.

8 Slide the martin gourd section over the spine and glue it in place. Set aside to dry.

9 Use the jigsaw to cut an opening in the gourd head big enough to insert the spine, and glue in place.

10 Cut more gourd stems, dip their ends in the glue and push the stems up under the neck. Keep adding stems until you have the desired effect.

11 If you wish, coat the finished gourd with spar varnish.

"I love, love, love gourds!" —Dyan Mai Peterson

Umbrella Woman

Has there ever been a garden figure more in love with the rain than this exquisite lady made from umbrella parts? For a burst of living color, let flowers twine around her skirt.

BEFORE YOU START

Tag sales are wonderful places to find umbrellas of all sizes. I found a large patio umbrella that had not one, but two, serviceable frames. Adjust the instruction measurements to suit your umbrellas.

INSTRUCTIONS

1 Remove the fabric from the umbrellas for the skirt and bodice sections.

2 Cut a circular base out of one of the plywood squares that is the diameter of the bottom spread of the skirt spokes. Place the umbrella on the circle, pencil marking the placement of each spoke on the circumference. Use the jigsaw to cut small notches for each spoke. Cut a hole in the center of the base to hold the center pole. Slide the skirt umbrella over the center pole. Depending on what the spoke material is (plastic or metal) adhere the spokes to the notches with glue, or screws.

3 Make the waist spacer between the skirt and the bodice from an appropriately sized plywood square with a center hole for the pole, such as the 6-inch (15.2 cm) square in the photo. Slip the spacer over the pole and rest it on the top of the skirt, turning it slightly so it looks like a diamond from the front. Later you'll use the spacer to add umbrella fabric to the skirt.

4 Make the bodice top. Cut a plywood circle 12 to 16 inches (30 to 40.5 cm) in diameter (with a center hole for the pole) so that it will fit snugly inside and flush to the spokes on the top of the bodice umbrella section when it is placed on the waist spacer. Secure the spokes to the bodice circle top, using fasteners appropriate to the spoke material.

Design by Merry Miller

MATERIALS

UMBRELLAS
* Salvaged umbrella shapes to make skirt, bodice, and hair spokes
* Patio chair umbrella with clamp handle
* Child's umbrella
* Fabric from salvaged umbrellas

WOOD
* 2 pieces of ¾-inch (1.9 cm) plywood sheets, 24 inches (61 cm) square, to cut for the base, waist spacer, and collar
* Large wooden pole (diameter and height appropriate to your umbrella center)
* 1 x 2 at least 36 inches (91 cm) long, for the shoulder
* ½-inch (1.3 cm) dia. dowel, cut to 14 inches (35.5 cm) to make raised arm
* ¼-inch (6 mm) dia., dowel, cut to 4 inches (10.2 cm) for collar support

Wood screws
Fasteners to attach spokes to wood, as needed
Spray primer
Spray paint, colors of your choice for umbrella frames and wooden parts
Plastic or crystal beads
20-gauge wire
1-inch-long brads
1 package of curly drinking straws
26-gauge wire
1 hose clamp
Carpet tacks

TOOLS

Jigsaw
Drill
Hole saw
Screwdriver

5 Cut the 1 x 2 shoulder unit to a proportionate length. (The one in the photo is 36 inches long [.9 m].) With the holesaw, cut out a semi-circle in the shoulder unit so it fits snugly against the center pole. Screw the shoulder unit into the back of the pole. For added stability, place one screw on either side of the pole and drive them down through the shoulder unit into the bodice top.

6 Make the upraised arm. Cut the ½-inch (1.3 cm) diameter dowel into an arm length proportionate to your figure. (The one in this project is 14 inches [35.6 cm] long.) Drill a hole through the dowel about 3 inches (7.6 cm) from the top, where you'll thread wire later to attach the child's umbrella. Screw the lower end of the dowel in an upright position at the end of the shoulder unit, as shown in the photo above. Cut two pieces of 1 x 2 scrap into two lengths: 2 ½ inches (6.4 cm) and 3 ½ inches (8.9 cm). Using the holesaw, make a ½-inch hole (1.3 cm) in the center of each scrap piece. Glue the smaller piece on top of the larger one and slide both down the upraised arm. Glue the pieces to the shoulder. The scraps provide added support to the arm and shoulder.

7 To her other shoulder, fasten a clamped-handle umbrella or hang an umbrella with a hooked handle. Poke small holes in the umbrella bottom for drainage.

8 Make the collar. Cut a 4-inch (10.2 cm) plywood square with a center hole for the pole. Drill a hole through the center pole about 4 inches (10.2 cm) above the shoulder unit and insert the ¼-inch (6 mm) dowel as a pin on which to rest the collar. Pound brads into the collar (as in photo on page 127) so you can hang decorations later.

9 Make the head. Draw an egg-shaped oval on the plywood, proportionate to your figure and cut it out with the jigsaw. The head in the photo is about 8 inches (20.3 cm) tall. Imagine ears on her head and drill holes from ear to ear, spaced evenly about 1 ½ inches (3.8 cm) apart to hold her hair spokes later. Drill and screw the head onto the front of the center pole, a few inches above the collar.

10 Prime the figure, then paint the color of your choice.

11 Using the photo above for guidance, make the hair. Insert and glue the spokes and curly plastic drinking straws.

12 Using the 26-gauge wire, hang the raindrop crystals or other jewels on the hair spokes and the edges of the collar.

13 Attach the child's umbrella to the raised arm. Slip the hose clamp on both the umbrella handle and upraised arm, but don't tighten it yet. Thread the 20-gauge wire through the hole in the arm and use it to wrap the umbrella handle to the arm. Tighten the hose clamp over the wire wrapping to hide it, as well as to increase the pressure holding the two pieces together. (See the photo on page 127.)

14 Fold over four squares of umbrella fabric and tack them to the waist spacer. (See photo opposite.)

" I love the mystery in this figure...with its many rigid lines, at first it seems static, then after a few minutes you see the breeze is moving the fabric and making the beads sparkle."
— Merry Miller

DESIGN TIP

Weight the figure with flowerpots or an attractive arrangement of rocks on the base.

Delicious Scarecrow

After the harvest, welcome the foraging birds
with a scarecrow who offers tasty treats—all the way
from head to toe.

BEFORE YOU START

Gather all your natural materials, and bring them to the site
where you're building the figure.

INSTRUCTIONS

1 Make an armature the height and shape you want with wood pieces attached
with wood screws or thick bamboo tied with wire.

2 Spiral thick wire (at least 8 mm) around the armature, making a sturdy frame
on which you can weave and hang materials. (Don't use poultry netting—it's
too thin.) Wear protective gloves; use wire cutters to cut, and pliers to bend and
twist the wire as needed.

3 Using the photo to guide you, cover the frame, placing the heavier materials on
the torso and legs, and the lighter materials on the arms. First add the foliage
and ivy, weaving it in and out of the wire so it's firmly attached. Wrap ears of corn,
and hang them around the figure's waist. Add a medallion of a sunflower saved
from the summer. Thread the thin wire through apples and nuts to make necklaces.
Add clusters of grapes. Turn one basket upside down as a hat, pressing it down to
hold wands of millet as hair. Use the craft knife to carve the face in the skin of the
pumpkin, and stick it on the top of the spine.

4 Hang the other basket in the crook of the figure's arm. The basket is too deep
to serve as a bird feeder, but it can store seed. Insert a rainproof box snugly into
the basket, and fill it with seed. Depending on the types of birds that come to the
site, sprinkle seed on the ground or layer some on top of the box.

5 Once the birds discover the tasty scarecrow, they'll quickly devour it, so fresh-
en the figure often with new corn, fruits,
and nuts. In winter, add suet, sunflower
seeds, and other treats rich in fat.

DESIGN TIP

In spring, remove traces of old
foliage and food. Decorate the
figure with fresh food and nesting
material, such as strips of burlap.
See Medieval Maid Birdfeeder on
page 98 for ideas.

MATERIALS

NATURAL INGREDIENTS
* Foliage from evergreens
and ivy
* Moss
* Corn husks
* Nuts and sunflowers
* Apples, grapes, and other
available fruit
* Pumpkin with long
stem for head

Old basket, for hat
Old basket to hang on arm
Waterproof seed box to fit
snugly into arm basket
Enough bamboo poles or
2 x 2s to make the figure
you want
Enough wood screws or tying
wire, as needed
Approx. 100 feet (30 m)
of 8-mm galvanized wire
Approx. 30 feet (9 m) of
20-mm galvanized wire

TOOLS

Saw
Hammer
Pruners
Protective gloves
Wire cutters
Pliers
Craft knife

SAFETY GEAR

Protective gloves

Design by
Joan K. Morris

MATERIALS

Copper pipe, 1/2-inch (1.3 cm) dia., 33 feet for the man, 9 feet (2.8 m) for the dog

Copper elbows, 90° angle, 1/2-inch (1.3 cm) dia., 6 for the man, 8 for the dog

Copper tees, 1/2-inch (1.3 cm) dia., 6 for the man, 10 for the dog

Plumber's adhesive (be sure the label indicates it's for copper)

Stainless steel window screen

24-gauge stainless steel wire, cut into 2-inch (5 cm) lengths

Copper foil, small sheet

Copper wire, 24 gauge

4 stainless steel scouring pads for man's hair and goatee

12 copper kitchen scouring pads for dog

Binder ring, 1 inch (2.5 cm) dia.

Dog leash of your choice

Small dog collar

Clear polyurethane spray (optional)

TOOLS

Steel wool

Graph paper and pencil

Measuring tape

Marking pen

Tube cutting tool

Tin snips or old scissors

Safety gloves

Wire cutters

Hammer and nail

Drill and metal drill bit

Copper-Pipe Man & Poodle

Copper plumbing pipe and everyday kitchen scouring pads shape this dapper gentleman and his perfectly pouffed poodle.

BEFORE YOU START

Prepare a working area on the ground or floor, and cover it with newspaper to prevent glue drips. Use the steel wool to remove any writing or dirt on the pipes.

INSTRUCTIONS

1 Using the photograph as a guide, draw your figures on the graph paper. (The man in the photo is 6 feet [2 m] tall; the dog, including its head, is 2 feet [61 cm] tall.) To each pipe leg, add a support pipe underground that is at least one-third the aboveground height of the figure.

2 Measure and mark each section of pipe, including the supports. Following the manufacturer's instructions on the tube cutter, cut each section.

3 Working from the head down, lay out all the sections, then join the straight pipe pieces with the copper elbows and copper tees, as needed. Dry fit as you go.

4 Once you're happy with all the fittings, glue the joints with the plumber's adhesive. Put the glue on the inside of the tees and elbows and slide the pipes into the glue, so it doesn't ooze out.

5 Leave the two pipes under the man's feet un-glued, so you can remove him from the ground.

6 Repeat the process with the poodle. Place a wad of newspaper under his ear to hold it out at an angle until the glue sets.

7 Let everything dry for 24 hours before accessorizing.

8 Using the photos to guide you, and wearing protective gloves, cut and fold sections of screen to make the vest and the pocket. Just as you'd tack a garment with preliminary stitches to hold it in place, tack the pocket to the vest with a piece of stainless steel wire and twist it in the back to secure it.

9 Make the buttons with four circles cut from the copper foil. Nail two holes in the center of each button. Tack the buttons in place with copper wire, twisting on the inside of the vest to close it.

10 Make the flower out of a strip of copper foil 2 by 10 inches (5 x 25.4 cm). On one of the long edges, cut out a petal pattern about every inch (2.5 cm). Starting at one end, roll the cut copper foil, flaring out the petals. Wrap the bottom with 10 inches (25.4 cm) of wire, and attach the flower to the pocket with the wire.

11 Make the man's hair and goatee with the stainless steel scouring pads. Open each one and spread it in a circle. Wrap three around the top of the man's head. Pull one or more wires out of each pad, and use them to tie the pads onto the head. Repeat with one scouring pad for his goatee.

12 Make the poodle fur with the copper scouring pads. Spread out three of the pads for the top of his head and back. For the ear, tail, and two legs, don't unfold the pads—keep them in their ball-shape, and wire them in place with a pulled wire, putting plumber's adhesive inside each one to hold it.

13 Drill a hole at the bottom of the man's outside hand, slip the binder ring through it to hold the leash, and attach the collar to the leash.

14 Keep the figures shiny by spraying them with clear polyurethane, or let them weather naturally.

15 Pound the support pipes into the ground and slip the figures into them.

DESIGN TIP

Poodles have many cuts. Make the simple "show" cut like the dog in the photo or go scrubbie-wild and make any poodle cut you want.

"I was doing dishes—and the copper scrubbies reminded me of my friend's French poodle. I laughed so hard I knew I had to make yard figures using scrubbies."—Joan K. Morris

Detail of Tim Fowler's *Tile Woman*.

Yard figures are prominent pieces in one of the first museum exhibits solely devoted to yard art. The *Yard Art* exhibit was on view at the Hallie Ford Museum of Art at Williamette University, Salem, Oregon, in the fall of 2003.

ALL PHOTOS COURTESY OF JOHN OLBRANTZ, THE MARTIBETH COLLINS DIRECTOR, PHOTOS BY DALE PETERSON, PORTLAND OREGON

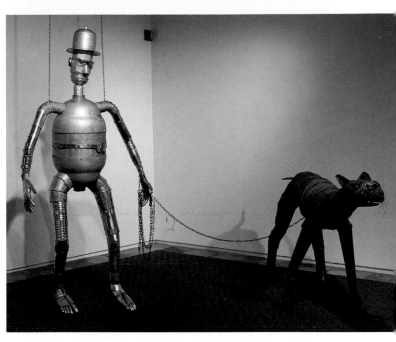

Man and Dog prove why artist Reid Peterson, from Enumclaw, Washington, is known for yard figures of a grand size and even bigger sense of humor. He favors using salvage metal for most of his pieces.

Tim Fowler, from Seattle, Washington, makes unique yard figures from heavy materials. *Tile Woman* (left) and *Garter Snake Birdbath* (center) are made from tile over mesh, with a frame of pvc pipes and rebar. *Rock Man* (right) is appropriately named.

Shorty on the Move (foreground), and *Balpeen Batter* (background), by Tim Fowler, are made from materials that other people use to build their patios.

Corn Harvest Thanksgiving

Design by Merry Miller

All summer the crow guardians kept their small brethren away from the garden. The corn grew tall and abundant. As thanksgiving, the Corn Goddess arrays herself in corncobs and offers them to the birds and animals.

BEFORE YOU START

You can make the crow feathers from any material that will move gently in the wind—wood, metal, plastic, even fabric. One of the crows in the photo was made with wood lattice, the other with plastic window blind slats painted black. Follow the general instructions below, substituting as needed for the materials you choose. To make more than one crow, just increase the materials accordingly.

INSTRUCTIONS
Crow with Wood Lattice Feathers

1 Make the feathers and sort in a separate pile for each wing. Cut 32 pieces, 16 for each wing, two of each length, labeling each piece on its bottom: 26, 25, 24, 23, 22, 21, 20, 19, 18, 17, 15, 13, 11, 9, 7, and 5 inches (66, 63.2, 61, 58.4, 55.8, 50.8, 48.3, 45.7, 43.2, 38.1, 33, 27.9, 22.9, 17,8, 12.7 cm).

2 Holding each piece by its bottom, and, being careful not to cover up the labels, spray the primer. Let dry. Spray black, again avoiding the labels, and let dry. (When fully assembled, you can paint the tips and do touch-ups.)

3 Prime and paint the body and wing support pieces.

4 Draw the crow's head—about 14 inches (35.5 cm) tall—on the plywood, and cut it out. Cut out an oval for the crow's eye. Prime and paint both sides.

5 Working on a flat surface, make a cross by placing the horizontal wing support behind the spine and far enough down to allow space for the crow's head. Screw the crosspieces together from behind.

6 Make one wing at a time. Beginning with the 26-inch (66 cm) feather and working from the center outward to the tip of the wing, arrange the feathers, placing the five feathers numbered 26 to 22 *underneath* the horizontal piece.

MATERIALS
for One Crow Guardian

7 wood lattice strips, 10 feet (3 m) long, or window blind strips, for feathers

1 x 2, 5 feet (1.5 m) long, for horizontal wing

2 x 2, 6 feet long (1.9 m), for the spine (save extra wood)

Circular color coding labels

Can of spray primer paint

Can of flat black spray paint

3/4-inch (1.9 cm) plywood, 24 inches (61 cm) square

Wood screws and nails

Ball of twine

Sheet of adhesive-backed black felt

Tiny screw eyes to hang eyes

Wire

Rebar, 4 feet (1.2 m) long

Sandpaper

Black carpet tacks

TOOLS
for Crow Guardian & Corn Goddess

Jigsaw

Drill with 7/32-inch (6 mm) bit

Screwdriver

Paintbrush

Measuring tape

Scissors

7 Make the edges flush, and drill holes through both the feather and wing support.

8 Place feathers 21 to 17 *on top* of the support. Match edges and drill holes through each piece.

9 Place the remaining feathers *underneath* the support, and drill their holes.

10 Attach each feather with a 10-inch (25.4 cm) piece of twine. Thread the twine from the front through the holes, and knot several times in the back.

11 Repeat for the opposite wing.

12 Nail the front of the crow's head into the spine.

13 Remove the colored labels. Prime and paint the tips of the feathers and all the areas that might need a touch-up. Trim and paint the twine knots, and spray them black.

14 Make movable pupils for the crow's eye with two equal-size circles cut from the black felt. Sandwich a tiny screw-eye stem between their adhesive sides, and press together. Insert another tiny screw eye into the top edge of the wooden eye hole. Wire the two screw eyes together so the pupil hangs freely—even the slightest breeze appears to make the crow's eye move in constant vigilance.

15 Attach the rebar to the spine support and insert into the ground.

INSTRUCTIONS
Crow with
Window Blind Feathers

In general, follow the same construction principles as the wood-feathered crow, starting on page 135, with these exceptions:

1 The widths of window blinds vary, so modify the measurements as needed. For example, instead of 16 wood pieces on each wing, the designer used 21 slender window blinds on each. Use scissors to cut the blinds to length.

2 Attach the blinds to the front of the wing support with carpet tacks. The blinds can't swing back and forth like the wooden lattice pieces, but they do occasionally move laterally, overlapping each other to create the illusion, from a distance, that the wings are moving in preparation for flight.

DESIGN TIP

Place crows in different parts of your garden, like benign sentinels.

MATERIALS
for Corn Goddess

2 x 2, 7 feet (2.1 cm) long, for the spine

1 x 2, 5 feet (1.5 m)long, for the horizontal support

Wood screws

³/4-inch (1.9 cm) thick plywood sheet, cut to 2 x 3 feet (.6 x .9 m)

Cans of spray paint, golden-orange

Clear exterior plumber's glue

30 to 40 cobs of Indian corn with husks

Twine

12-inch (31 cm) round metal wreath support

20-gauge wire

Raffia ribbon

Rebar, 4 feet (1.2 m) long

INSTRUCTIONS
Corn Goddess

1 Make the body support by crossing the two pieces of lumber. Attach the horizontal piece with wood screws about 5 inches (13 cm) from the top of the spine, creating the illusion of a very tall figure.

2 Using the photo on page 134 to guide you, draw the shield-shaped body on the plywood. Cut out the shape with the jigsaw.

3 Paint the body and let it dry.

4 Glue the corncobs onto the body in a pattern that shows off their colors. Trim the cornhusks as you wish, but save them to make the hands— glue layers of husks on the end of the arms, and bind them with twine.

5 Attach the metal wreath head. Drill two holes on the spine, spaced about ½-inch (1.3 cm) apart, about 2 inches (5 cm) from the top. Thread wire through the holes, and twist to secure the head. Wrap raffia around the neck to cover the wire, and weave a zigzag pattern for hair decoration. Slip in a feather or other ornament.

6 The corn goddess will be quite heavy, so attach the rebar to her spine before you insert her into the ground.

"I was inspired to create this project by Cherokee legends, which portray humans in a grateful relationship with the animals and birds." — Merry Miller

137

Navajo scarecrows deter crows as well as coyotes and wolves who prey on the tribe's sheep. An old steering wheel makes this figure's head.

An old tin bucket makes a head. As the seasons pass, clothing is often taken down and assembled into a new scarecrow.

Because the Navajos consider it taboo to make a scarecrow look human, there are never any facial features on their figures.

PHOTO BY NANCY HUNTER WARREN

ALL PHOTOS ON THIS PAGE COURTESY OF THE PHOTOGRAPHER, NANCY HUNTER WARREN, SANTA FE, NEW MEXICO

A flirty metal "Bathing Beauty" goddess serves as the base for a birdbath.

"Athena" on her chariot is an example of the classical images that take on contemporary forms in today's yard figures.

Giant natural figures, especially insects such as "French Flight," are favorite themes with outdoor artists.

ALL PHOTOS ON THIS PAGE COURTESY OF THE ARTIST, KIM MERRIMAN, OLYMPIA, WASHINGTON. SHE IS A METAL ARTIST WHO USES STAINED GLASS IN MANY OF HER DESIGNS.

Contributing Designers

Harry Abel takes pride in the distinctive choices and intricate handiwork that make each of his Japanese-inspired garden creations unique. He is an associate master and teacher of Japanese flower arranging and Ikebana. Harry works all over the country drawing on his diverse background "…to translate beauty into useable art forms." His work has appeared in *The Craft & Art of Bamboo* (Lark Books, 2001). He lives in Smyrna, Georgia. shishi@aol.com, www.shinkigen.com

Stacey Budge is an art director at Lark Books. When she is not hard at work designing beautiful books, such as *Nursery Rhyme Knits* and *The Art of French Beaded Flowers* (Lark Books, 2004), she can be found enjoying the relaxing pursuits of gardening and knitting at her home in Asheville, North Carolina.

John Buettner, an accomplished illustrator and graphic designer, produces nature-inspired projects for zoos, museums, field guides, and textbooks. This is his first Lark book. John migrated from the prairies of Oklahoma to Raleigh, North Carolina, where he currently divides his time between working at a small publishing company and participating in local gardening events. johnbuettner@hotmail.com

William Drake recycles metal into distinctive art. A self-taught blacksmith, he enjoys crafting replica medieval weapons out of everyday items such as railroad spikes and horseshoes. This is his first Lark book. William is the owner of Deep in the Woods Forge and lives with his wife, Marlene, and a menagerie of animals in Fairview, North Carolina. deepinthawoods@hotmail.com

Cynthia Gillooly loves flowers. Her passions have blossomed into a two-decade career in the floral design industry and her designs have been published in more than a dozen Lark books, including *Arranging Silk Flowers* (2003). She is currently a commercial orchid grower. Cynthia lives in Alexander, North Carolina, where she manages her greenhouse and her design firm. Skywatcher678@aol.com

Mary Hettmansperger is a fiber artist who works in basketry, beadwork, and metals. She has been a full-time educator for more than 20 years and teaches in all venues of fiber art. Her works have been featured in national galleries, juried shows, and art publications, including *Fiberarts Design Book 7* (Lark Books, 2004). Mary will be authoring a book on making jewelry with basket weaving techniques to be published by Lark Books in 2005. She lives with her husband and children on a farm in Peru, Indiana. hetts@ctlnet.com

Jimmy Hopkins credits his family for much of his creative inspiration. His distinctive works are fashioned from a variety of found-metal treasures, including vintage tools, automobile parts, and old farm equipment. Jimmy sells his pieces at art shows across the southeast and in retail shops in Atlanta and Asheville. His work was featured in *Salvage Style for the Garden* (Lark Books, 2003). He lives outside Atlanta, Georgia. www.creativemetalcreations.com

Diana Light takes many of her artistic inspirations from myths and nature. She is an accomplished painter and printmaker. Her singular designs have been featured in a wide variety of Lark Books titles, including *Decorating with Mini-Lights* and *Salvage Style for the Garden*. She is the author of *The Weekend Crafter: Etching Glass* (Lark Books, 2000) and *The Weekend Crafter: Batik* (Lark Books, 2004) She resides in Weaverville, North Carolina, where she often takes a break from creating to swim with the mermaids. dianalight@hotmail.com

Merry Miller is a professional portrait painter, muralist, and free-lance graphic artist. Though formally trained, Merry prefers to "break rules and play" in the construction of her inventive assemblage pieces. She hails from a talented family of creative parents and quirky siblings. This is her first Lark book, for which she designed 12 projects and drew the illustrations. Merry resides in her birthplace of Cleveland, Ohio. merrymillerdesign@earthlink.net

Nathalie Mornu works and plays in Asheville, North Carolina. In addition to her tableware-inspired project for this book, she has crafted designs for other Lark Books titles, including *Decorating Your First Apartment* (2002) and *Gingerbread Houses* (2004).

Joan Morris has been a creative contributor to many Lark Books titles including, *Beautiful Ribbon Crafts* (2003) and *Hardware Style* (2003) and is the author of *The Weekend Crafter: Simple Upholstery* (2004). Her artistic pursuits have led her down a number of diverse paths, including motion picture costuming and ceramic design. Joan is currently the proud owner of Vincent's Ear, a landmark coffeehouse in Asheville, North Carolina.

Pamela Owens, CBA, is the owner of Bravo Events, an event planning/balloon decorating business in Asheville, North Carolina. She earned her certified balloon artist status, an international certification, in 1995. She has won many trade show décor awards, including the Carolinas International Special Events Society award for Best Balloon Design Event in 2001. This is her first Lark book.
www.bravoevents.com

Emma Pearson earned her art and design degree from Bretton Hall College in Yorkshire, England, before moving to the States. This Welsh-born artist enjoys crafting jackets and hats that are practical and fun, with an element of her "pixie." Her work has appeared in several Lark Books titles, including *Halloween: A Grown-Up's Guide to Creative Costumes, Devilish Décor & Fabulous Festivities* (2003) and *The Artful Cupcake* (2004). She lives in western North Carolina and creates from her studio, Pelly Fish Design. pellyfish@yahoo.com.

Dyan Mai Peterson is an internationally known gourd artist, teacher, and author of *The Decorated Gourd* (Lark Books, 2002). Her artwork has been featured in numerous books and magazines. In addition to her passion for gourd craft, Dyan is an accomplished basket weaver and mixed media artist. She and her husband, furniture maker Gary Peterson, live on a gourd farm in the beautiful mountains of Burnsville, North Carolina.
Dyanmai.Peterson@verizon.net
www.thedecoratedgourd.com

Simon and Christi Whiteley are the owners of Eldorado Architectural Salvage & Antiques, an upscale architectural elements shop in Hendersonville, North Carolina. The Whiteleys offer an unusual inventory of reclaimed items they've bought, collected, and restored. Together with their new daughter Vivian and their dogs, Maevis and Jock, they sleuth everywhere for good stuff that others overlook. A dozen of their unique designs are featured in *Salvage Style for the Garden* (Lark Books, 2003).
esalvage@bellsouth.net

Terry Taylor lives and works in Asheville, North Carolina, as an editor and a project coordinator for Lark Books. He is a prolific designer and exhibiting artist, and works in media ranging from metals and jewelry to paper crafts and mosaics. Some of the most recent Lark books to which he has contributed include *Creative Outdoor Lighting, Summer Style*, and *The Book of Wizard Craft*. He is the author of *Artful Eggs*.

Sandy Whittley, from San Angelo, Texas, has 8 children and 16 grandchildren—good reason to be a "Wild Woman of Spirit!" She's a creative jack-of-all-trades, with her artistic interests ranging from wood and metal work to contemporary art dolls and quilting. She enlists her husband, Hubert, to help her with the construction of her "out of the box" creations. This is her first Lark book. whittley@wcc.net

Author **Marcianne Miller** comes to book writing via previous careers in broadcasting and archaeology. She is the author of eight Lark Books, including *Salvage Style for the Garden* (2003), *Arranging Silk Flowers* (2003), and *The Artful Cupcake* (2004). She lives in Asheville, North Carolina, with her family and a furry menagerie. Every October her front yard is populated with scarecrows and yard figures.

Acknowledgments

We are stuffed with gratitude for all the scarecrow lovers who helped create this book.

Those closest to home
Merry Miller, project designer and illustrator
Caroline Jaynes-Winslow, patient neighbor
Elisabeth B. Miller, storyteller
Lonnie Darr, sweetheart

All the wildly creative project designers, who hail from Georgia, Indiana, North Carolina, Ohio, and Texas. See their snapshot bios on page 140.

The Artful Lark Books Team
Art Director Susan McBride
Principal Photographer Keith Wright
(www.keithwright.com)

Additional Photographers
Evan Bracken, John Dole, Stephen J. Salmon, Sandra Stambaugh, and Sanoma Syndication photographers Eric van Lokven, Jan Vermeer, and Hans Zeegers
Cover Designer Barbara Zaretsky
Fellow editor Terry Krautwurst, whose idea it was

Editorial Team Members
Rebecca Lim, Delores Gosnell, Rosemary Kast, Anne Hollyfield, Chris Winebrenner, and especially Assistant Editor Nathalie Mornu, whose efficient, unending helpfulness made the book happen
Editorial interns
Robin Heimer, Kailin E. Siegwald,
Ryan Sniatecki
Associate Art Directors Lance Willie
and Shannon Yokeley
Location Coordinator Jeff Hamilton

Asheville neighbors who graciously opened their gardens to us
Mark Burleson and Tom Metcalf
Ben Gillum and Heather Rayburn
Susan McBride
Sandra Yost of The Botanical Gardens At Asheville

The designers, photographers, and scarecrow festival organizers who generously contributed photographs to the Basics and Gallery sections of the book, so we could show you the truly international scope of scarecrows and yard figures
Rose O'Brien and all the scarecrow designers of the Mahone Bay Scarecrow Festival, Mahone Bay, Nova Scotia

Janine Perey, Bernard Perey, and the Societé de l'Epouvantail, Denens, Switzerland

Sato Shinji, president of the Japanese Scarecrow Society, and author of *Kakashi*, a history of Japanese scarecrows and the Kaminoyama Hot Springs National Scarecrow Festival held at The Inn of Japan in Koyo

Hannah Nendick-Mason of the Cleveland Botanical Garden in Ohio and designers Eva Pawlak and Alison Wilson Kathleen Loubsky, Patty Thayer, and photographer Kathy Smith of the St. Charles Scarecrow Festival, St. Charles, Illinois

Bonnie Sierlecki, Jeff Olson, and designers from the Scarecrow Festival and the Flake Out Festival, Wisconsin Dells, Wisconsin

Susan K. Collins of the The Marshall Scarecrow Festival, Marshall, Michigan

Laurie Prax and designers of the Frosty Fever Festival, Valdez, Alaska

The art collectors and historians whose photographs showed the growing appreciation of scarecrows as folk art
John Olberantz, Curator of the Hallie Ford Museum of Art at Willamette University, Salem, Washington, and artists from the 2003 Yard Art Exhibit, Tim Fowler (p. 133), and Reid Peterson (p. 133)

Carl Hammer of Carl Hammer Gallery in Chicago, Illinois, (www.hammergallery.com) and photographer James Prinz (jamesprinz@earthlink.net)

John Foster of ENVISION Folk Art of Missouri, fosterdesign@charter.net

The scarecrow and yard figure artists and photographers whose work graced the book's gallery sections
Nancy Hunter Warren, photographer of the Navajo scarecrows (p. 138), which first appeared in El Palacio, The Magazine of the Museum of New Mexico, Cheryle Mano Mitchell, Managing Editor

Kim Merriman, metal and stained glass designer (p. 130), in Olympia, Washington, www.goddessgardenart.com

Jimmy Hopkins, Georgia salvage metal artist, (p. 90, 97) metalgardenart@yahoo.com

Big Bugs sculptor Dave Rogers (p. 105) from Glenwood Landing, New York, and photographer Harry Grod

Jane Orleman and Dick Elliott, who love visits from fellow yard figure artists at Dick & Jane's Spot, their home in Ellensburg, Washington (p.11), spot@ellensburg.com

The helpful people in Asheville, North Carolina
The many sales associates at Michael's, Home Depot, Lowe's, and B.B. Barnes who answered all our questions on the various craft, building, and garden supplies we needed to take our projects from rough idea to finished figure

The managers of Best Kept Secrets, Animal Haven Thrift Store, and the Goodwill Industries Retail Store for helping us find charming scarecrow outfits and goofy sunglasses

Junior League of Asheville's Not-So-New Shop, Manager Richard Fast, for the generous loan of the vintage cider jugs for our Junction City Jug Band project

Lastly, thanks to Edna, Hazel, Freddie, Barney, Buddy, Henry, Fannie, Chester, and Leroy, who sniffed, swatted, crawled in or climbed up all our scarecrows-in-the making, but damaged nary a one

Index

Notes about Suppliers

Usually, the supplies you need for making the projects in Lark books can be found at your local craft supply store, discount mart, home improvement center, or retail shop relevant to the topic of the book. Occasionally, however, you may need to buy materials or tools from specialty suppliers. In order to provide you with the most up-to-date information, we have created a listing of suppliers on our website, which we update on a regular basis. Visit us at www.larkbooks.com; click on "Craft Supply Sources"; and then click on the relevant topic. You will find numerous companies listed with their website address and/or mailing address and phone number.